A PATH TOO NARROW?

A Memoir of Improbable Journeys

J. TIMOTHY JOHNSON

Published by M.I.T. Johnson
Atlanta, GA
Copyright ©2025 by J. Timothy Johnson

First printing 2025

Cover design & book interior by Rick Robbins

ISBN 979-8-218-88755-1 Paperback

One need not hope in order to undertake,
nor succeed in order to persevere.

William the Silent
Dutch statesman and revolutionary leader (1533–1584)

Quoted by Guy Johnson in a letter
to his son Tim dated December 1, 1977

CONTENTS

CONTENTS

PREFACE

I was born and raised in an international Christian pacifist commune, the Bruderhof. It wasn't until my mid-teen years that I began to realize just how different my life was compared to others with whom I increasingly came into contact. I also realized then the difference was due to my parents' choice, before my birth, to join the Bruderhof shortly before the outbreak of WWII, embarking on a life path very different from that of their own parents or of the society in which they'd been raised, an improbable journey very different from even their own expectations.

In my teens, and on another continent, I was cast adrift by the commune into which I'd been born, the start of my own improbable journey. Three years later, my parents also left with their younger offspring. What had happened in the more than twenty years after my parents committed themselves to this community and its ideals of a pacifist, international, Christian "community of goods"?

Though I often considered this question, I rarely thought about chronicling my family's improbable journey until, in adulthood, I realized how often I was asked about my own improbable journey.

With regard to my parents' story, part of my reluctance to tell it was that I hoped my dad, Guy Johnson, would do so himself. While always ambivalent about it, he had not closed the door to the idea entirely. Sadly, he died much too soon at age sixty-five with no such manuscript though he, and to a lesser extent my mother, Eleanor, often talked of those earlier years at the Bruderhof.

As for my own story, I've been asked about my unusual background, and how that led me into a rewarding career completely different from anything I could have contemplated as a young child in a commune. Since much of my story was rooted in my parents' earlier choices, might one link the two into a joint narrative? Several of my siblings and colleagues encouraged me to engage in such an effort. Yet why me (and not one of my siblings) and why now, so many decades after the launching of my parents' sojourn?

Guy and Eleanor Johnson with their eight children and his mother,
Grannie John, at Wheathill shortly before the family departed for
the United States in 1955.

The eight children of Guy and Eleanor Johnson are themselves now getting on in years, and intimations of mortality are a potent impetus to reflection on family and personal journeys. I thus have been persuaded, as the eldest and having a memory that extends a little further back in our parents' lives than those of my siblings, to try to knit together a family history, beginning when our parents embarked on their Bruderhof journey together around the time that Europe stumbled into the Second World War. That history is the focus of the first section of this volume.

Central to it is, of course, the story of my parents — the life they established in their twenty-plus years living in communes in England, Paraguay, and the United States, and in the twenty-plus years back home in England after those utopian dreams shattered. They themselves wrestled continuously, yet mostly optimistically, with questions of "What's it all about?" and "Where do we go from here?" when expected avenues were unexpectedly blocked. They were bitterly disappointed that their vision of a twentieth-century life in a community patterned on their interpretation of the earliest Christian churches, as described in the New Testament's Acts of the Apostles, was ultimately found so badly wanting. Yet, after their return to England and adopting a seemingly more conventional life for their family, they continued to seek meaning in their lives, even as they examined what had failed in the efforts to live in an international "community of goods" bound by a common faith.

In those earlier years, they became the parents of lively and rather individualistic children who had not always conformed to their parents' hopes and expectations of becoming enthusiastic, or at least accepting, participants in their parents' communal life visions. Were Guy and Eleanor frustrated and disappointed when some of their children chose not to follow their parents' path? I don't know, but I think they accepted and understood the need of each of their children to find or develop his or her own meaning in life, much as they themselves had. I also think that by the 1960s they increasingly recognized that the Bruderhof, while retaining the name and many of its earlier values, had, like the world in which it was embedded, changed.

I hope to provide insight into those changes in both the Bruderhof and in my own thinking, especially during the turbulent years from about 1955 to 1961, when my parents were expelled back into a world they thought they'd left behind in 1938. By 1961, several of their older children, myself included, had also left or been expelled. Yet, I believe at some level they came to recognize that parts of their own deferred dreams might be realized through their children, geographically and temporally scattered though they had become.

The focus in the second half of this volume shifts to my journey after my unexpectedly hasty departure from the Bruderhof in 1958. I had only infrequent direct contact with my parents from that time onward and saw little of them after they and my younger siblings left the Bruderhof, returning soon to England in 1961. However, our parents did their best (in our pre-internet world) to stay in contact with those of us remaining in the United States. In particular, I could expect a thoughtful annual greeting around the time of my birthday. It is from one of these messages that I'll conclude this prologue, with some excerpted musings by my dad, in a letter written to me on October 10, 1977, sixteen months before he passed away.

Dad reminisces about a walk he and I had on the Sussex Downs, during which we'd discussed the question posed by science fiction authors and futurists of "where do we go from here?"

I don't think it matters really that none of us has the answer. What does matter is the comradeship that so often grows up between those who sincerely ask the question — and who, through thick and thin, go on asking it, even though they frequently find themselves at odds with those — and they are the majority — who tend (and who doesn't some of the time?) to accept supinely the status quo without question — and particularly if it provides a fairly comfortable environment.

At this point, Dad imagines hearing a demurral on behalf of his master from our dog, Boswell, with whom Dad had established a friendly bond during a visit to us in Ann Arbor a couple of years earlier. Dad responds:

"OK, Bos, you have a point. But I am grateful for the many times your Master has gone out of his way to make an enquiry of one of his siblings how they are faring in this hard world. One of the things that warms my heart when thinking of our family is that though they are a funny lot and, in their astonishing diversity frequently get on each other's nerves, there is something that binds them together."

Boswell, Eleanor, Carol, and
Guy Johnson – Upper Peninsula, Michigan,
October 1975

This volume is a celebration of Guy and Eleanor Johnson and of their eight children, each of whom traveled parts of Guy and Eleanor's improbable journey with them.

In chronological birth order, Guy and Eleanor's children are: John Timothy (Tim), Joy Barbara, Barnabas David, Susan Mary, Elizabeth Ann, Jane Elfriede (Elfie), Christrose Carol (Rosie), and Rebecca Eleanor.

While this narrative focuses on my parents and me, it is also, in part, my siblings' story, as we each carried forward, in our own ways and on our own paths, the legacy of our parents and their active, thoughtful, questioning approach to life: "What's it all about?" and "Where do we go from here?"

Author's note: Stamps as Messengers

Interspersed with the photos in my narrative are postage stamps. Why?

First, a practical reason. There are very few photos available from my early years, including, notably, my early life in Paraguay, my teen and preteen years in England, and my "North Dakota/Hutterites" period. (Photographs were regarded as "graven images" and banned by the Hutterites in those early days. A great pity, in retrospect.)

The lack of access to cameras (due to shortage of money for such frivolity!) extended for some years into my "post-Bruderhof expulsion" period. Even in my later life, circumstances sometimes meant I had little access to photographic records.

Second, a more subtle reason — I realized that my somewhat informal but almost lifelong collection of postage stamps could both partially offset the lack of personal photographs and complement my story in both direct and maybe more indirect ways. Part of my story is historical and geographical, and stamps can reflect both history and geography.

Also, stamps came to serve as a limited yet important connection to my paternal grandfather and avid stamp collector, Edward D. Johnson. Due to our family's earlier life away from England, along with substantial differences in political and religious philosophies between my dad and grandfather, I'd unfortunately had very little direct contact in my early years with my grandfather. Yet after I started collecting stamps, a bit of a bond developed between us, mainly through his own well-established interest in stamps and their stories. I found he was a fount of knowledge and good advice on stamps and the stories they told and how to present them. This discovery, as well as other interests he exposed us to, contributed to a gradual appreciation of the lives lived by our parents' parents, and our wider circle of non-Bruderhof relatives more generally. Certainly, I began to appreciate better what our own nuclear family had missed by largely withdrawing from our outside-world families

in favor of ties almost solely within the community of co-believers. Stamps provided for me, and perhaps other young Bruderhofers, a view beyond the commune walls.

My selection of stamps used as illustrations in this book was informally guided (besides the availability of suitable specimens in my own collection) by a several factors. I wanted these stamps to reflect aspects of our journeyings, including our family's life in Paraguay, England, and within the United States. Stamps commemorating the states I became particularly familiar with are highlighted. So are commemoratives, which spoke to the history and other aspects of our new home and world, or in some cases, to personally important developments.

For my post-Bruderhof life, I've selected stamps from countries in which I was particularly involved, either in terms of time lived there or multiple working visits over extended time periods.

Collectively, I hope the stamps contribute something to my overall story and perhaps allow readers' minds to speculatively fill in some of the gaps I've left!

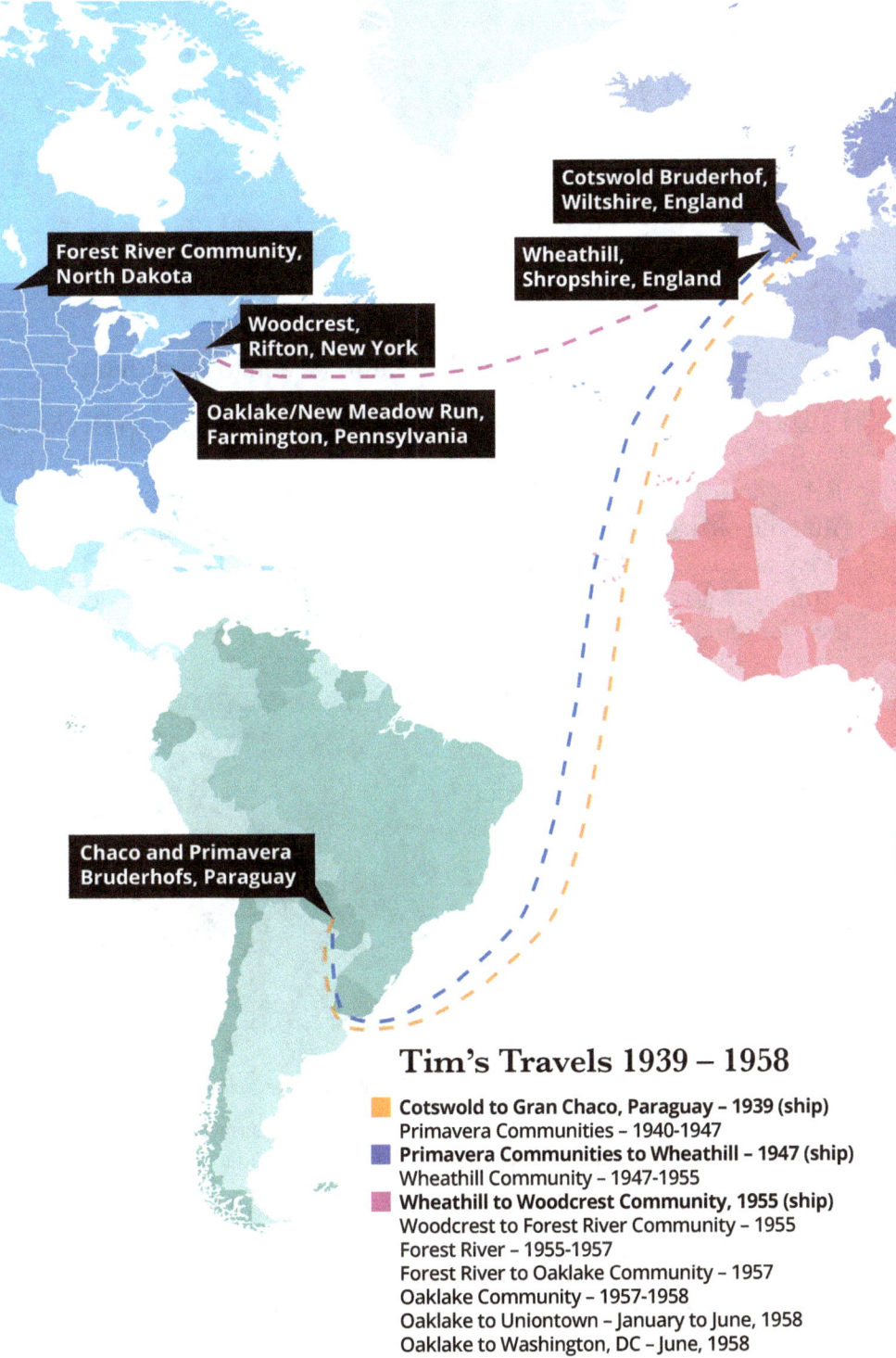

Forest River Community,
North Dakota

Woodcrest,
Rifton, New York

Oaklake/New Meadow Run,
Farmington, Pennsylvania

Cotswold Bruderhof,
Wiltshire, England

Wheathill,
Shropshire, England

Chaco and Primavera
Bruderhofs, Paraguay

Tim's Travels 1939 – 1958

Cotswold to Gran Chaco, Paraguay – 1939 (ship)
Primavera Communities – 1940-1947
Primavera Communities to Wheathill – 1947 (ship)
Wheathill Community – 1947-1955
Wheathill to Woodcrest Community, 1955 (ship)
Woodcrest to Forest River Community – 1955
Forest River – 1955-1957
Forest River to Oaklake Community – 1957
Oaklake Community – 1957-1958
Oaklake to Uniontown – January to June, 1958
Oaklake to Washington, DC – June, 1958

Part One

THE BRUDERHOF YEARS

Chapter 1 – Before January 1939
The English Midlands

It is best, I believe, to begin with an introduction to my parents.

Eleanor Elizabeth Dutton, "Eleanor," my mother, was born on December 4, 1912, along with her twin sister, Audrey Ann, to Benjamin and Mary (Bebington) Dutton of Kelsall, a small rural town in Cheshire, England. After the birth of the twins, Benjamin and Mary had two more daughters, Mary and Ettie, and then a son, Tom. The family also included Wesley, a son, born to Benjamin and his first wife before her untimely death, and therefore an older half brother to my mother and her siblings.

After their school years in Kelsall, and then in the large county seat of Chester, my mother and Audrey Ann left for London, where they both trained to be teachers at Southlands College, a Methodist Church institution near Wimbledon. Despite being very close and together to this point, the twin sisters went to different locations for their initial teaching positions. Eleanor went to teach in Birmingham, England, the major Midlands industrial city, in a rather underprivileged area.

Eleanor Dutton visiting Dudley Castle in the West Midlands, 1930s

This choice was intentional. She wanted to be more exposed to youngsters from a background different from her own middle-class one — an early sign of social activism on her part. It was in Birmingham, England at Carrs Lane Congregational Church that she met my father.

Edward Guy Johnson, "Guy," my father, was born September 21, 1913, in Birmingham, England, to Edward D. and Marguerite "Daisy" (Owen) Johnson. Guy's elder sister, Barbara, was born in 1911 and his younger brother, David, was born in 1917.

The family could be considered upper middle class and was well established in the city. My father's schooling included Uppingham School, a boarding school then just for boys, in nearby Rutland County. He was later joined there by his brother, David.

After Uppingham, Guy attended the University of Birmingham, where he trained as a solicitor (lawyer). He then joined his father's law firm in Birmingham, though as he described it, not with great enthusiasm. As with

Guy Johnson September 1931

many young folks of his interwar generation, he found himself increasingly dissatisfied with the society into which he had been born. What should his response be to the social disparities around him? What was his position regarding rising militarism, and the rising opposition to it, as European nations struggled with the consequences of the Great Depression, increased nationalism, and the threats posed particularly by Germany and Nazism? Social ferment was widespread among young people, and along the way, Guy found himself active with other young people who saw possible solutions in radical, but non-militaristic, Christianity. Guy was a member of Carrs Lane Congregational Church and the minister, Rev. Leyton Richards, had a national reputation as a pacifist who preached that the Gospel must be applied in all aspects of life, in personal, public, and international affairs. This thinking eventually led Guy, along with Eleanor, who was moving in the same circles, to his first exposure to the Bruderhof, a group committed to a pacifist Christian vision of peaceful coexistence with people of other nationalities who shared these views.

What was this group of communitarians to whom Eleanor and Guy were increasingly attracted?

A Brief History of the Bruderhof – 1920 to 1938

The Bruderhof began in Germany in 1920. Though still comprising only a few families and single adults, by 1923 it was a fully established commune, the Rhön Bruderhof, close to the city of Fulda. It was spawned in the social and religious ferment of post World War I European dissatisfaction with existing societal structures. Among several groups of young seekers of better ways to organize society was the international Anabaptist-pacifist Bruderhof, founded by Eberhard Arnold and others in Germany. This group sought to apply their interpretation of the practices of the early Christian church communities, notably a communal life, with radical non violence. In this, they were guided by early Anabaptist writings, including those of the Hutterites, an Anabaptist sect originating in the Tyrol region around 1527 and derived from the Swiss Brethren. The Hutterites are formally considered to have been established in 1528, when the much-persecuted group emigrated from Tyrol to Moravia under their soon-to-be-martyred leader, Jakob Hutter, for whom the sect came to be named.[1]

The Bruderhof soon discovered that some of the Hutterites, who had been in a long decline in eastern Europe (now Ukraine) following their expulsion from Bohemia and Moravia, had reestablished themselves in North America in the 1870s, and by the 1930s had thriving agrarian communities (colonies) in the northern United States and in some of the prairie provinces of Canada. In the early 1930s, the Bruderhof's founder, Eberhard Arnold, visited North America, and, after about a year, returned to Germany as a newly anointed minister (in German, *Prediger, Diener-am-Wort,* or, in English, "Servant of the Word") in the Hutterian church. By this time, 1932, the total population of the Rhön Bruderhof had reached one hundred adults and children, with several European nationalities represented, in an increasingly xenophobic Germany. Subsequently, two Hutterite ministers reciprocated Eberhard Arnold's North American trip with a visit to the young German Rhön Bruderhof. While this exchange helped cement the formal relationship, it also revealed substantial differences between the two groups.

Nazi harassment had already led the Bruderhof in 1934 to establish an outpost in politically neutral Liechtenstein. The Alm Bruderhof was a safe haven for particularly vulnerable members, including young German men

---

[1] This section is adapted in part from an article by J. Timothy Johnson and Ruth Lambach, "A Community of Bruderhof Leavers: Reflections on the KIT/Hummer Process" in *Communal Societies*, vol. 33, no. 2, 2013, 161–180

of military conscription age. Then, in a severe blow to the young commune, its founder, Eberhard Arnold, died unexpectedly during surgery on November 22, 1935, just as the Bruderhof was wrestling with both internal crises and issues of survival in the Nazi state.

In England, the emerging interest in the Bruderhof message combined with a concern for what was happening in Germany led to the founding of the Cotswold Bruderhof near Ashton Keynes, Wiltshire, in 1936. Recognizing Nazi political trends, members and their families of the Rhön Bruderhof began to flow from Germany to the Cotswold Bruderhof, also in 1936. The exodus swelled after the Rhön Bruderhof was dissolved by the Nazi Gestapo (secret police) on April 14, 1937, and its members expelled. Most traveled to and regrouped in the new Cotswold Bruderhof by 1938.

Carrs Lane Church – 1930s, Birmingham, England

Carrs Lane Church was at this time a progressive Congregational church near the Bull Ring market in central Birmingham, England and both Guy and his mother were active members.

In 1935, at the youthful age of twenty-one, Guy had become a deacon at Carrs Lane. Around this same time, and with assistance of friends who were familiar both with political developments in Nazi Germany and with the serious problems it presented for the pacifist Bruderhof, "Hardi" Arnold, the eldest son of the founder of the Bruderhof movement in Germany, came to Birmingham, England to study at the University of Birmingham and avoid Nazi militarism and conscription. In part through a connection with Hardi, a few young people from the church visited the Rhön Bruderhof, and a young couple, Gladys and Arnold Mason, joined that community in Germany. They had been part of the circle of young activists at Carrs Lane. This circle, called the Seventy Club and named for the New Testament account of Jesus sending forth seventy apostles to spread his gospel, was led first by Godfrey Pain, and after his departure, was led by Guy.

Perhaps the earliest mention of the Bruderhof with reference also to Guy and Eleanor occurs in 1935. Nancy Watkins (later, Trapnell), a young member of the Seventy Club at that time, writes in her reminiscences more than fifty years later of a church meeting that Eberhard, with

Hardi serving as his interpreter, was invited to address. I give here several excerpts from her account, both for historic interest and because, despite some vagueness that crept in over the intervening years, Nancy provides a nice review of what was going on in that group at the time:[2]

Guy's mother was a member of Carrs Lane in which her son had just been named a Deacon. She knew of this meeting but could not attend on the selected day. So, Guy unsuspiciously walks up to his mother and says, 'Oh, Mother, does that mean you'll not be using the car?' 'No,' she says, 'take it.' So, Guy hops into the car and goes around to a few places and picks up Eleanor, scoots across town and picks up me . . . we arrived at the church late. So, we walked in and sat at the back of the conference room.

Eberhard was on the platform standing, his leg in a cast [and] supporting himself with a stick. Hardi was standing by him, translating . . . Then they adjourned to the vestry, so we moved along [to] the door. When w e got there, there were two elderly deacons. 'Oh,' they said, 'this is not for the young people.' We were so taken aback that we couldn't open our mouths . . . The only one allowed in was Guy, because he was 'a deacon!'

Nancy goes on to report how, in the following year, the young members of the church collectively moved toward the Bruderhof. She notes, "Once, Guy Johnson took me to the Cotswold to deliver a vanload of used items that had been collected at Carrs Lane for the new community." This delivery apparently occurred in 1936 and is the first actual mention of a visit to the Cotswold Bruderhof by members of the Seventy Club.

In August 1936, Nancy reported, Guy, "a lawyer," with "a certain standing" was asked by some of the young members of the church to "look for a house in a poor neighborhood (in Birmingham, England) where we could begin to live and share together." This request resulted, in early 1937, in the establishment of the Handsworth New Road Community House.

Residents of the house included Guy Johnson, Eleanor Dutton (later Johnson), Lloyd Jones, Howard Cheney, Francis Beels, Sylvia Walker (later Beels). Nancy's elderly parents, Jabez and Elizabeth Watkins, agreed to become the "house parents" and Nancy took responsibility for cooking and cleaning while the others were out working their regular jobs.

[2]The reminiscences, my only direct reference from this period, were shared with me by Mark Trapnell, Nancy's son.

In 1937, the Handsworth community members visited the Cotswold Bruderhof for the Whitsun weekend. This visit unexpectedly resulted in the invitation to consider themselves novices within that community. They did and henceforth called their community house the "Bruderhof House."

Further individual and group visits to the Cotswold Bruderhof eventually led to the resignation from Carrs Lane of these young members as they transferred their allegiance to the Bruderhof.[3]

Carrs Lane Church's senior pastor was Leyton Richards, who had visited both the Rhön Bruderhof and its outpost in Liechtenstein, the Alm Bruderhof. The Bruderhof's radical interpretation of Christianity, as something to be lived rather than studied or just believed, appealed to him. Yet he also felt there were other ways to express and live one's Christian faith, as he described in part in the church bulletin from 1938. In it, Leyton Richards discussed the resignation of some Carrs Lane Church members who had decided to join with the Bruderhof's Cotswold community.

The announcement of these resignations is worth excerpting verbatim. Though naming only Guy among the several young members who chose to leave, Leyton Richards's announcement shows not only the high regard he had for Guy, and respect for his decision, but also the pain of the separation:

Message from Rev. Leyton Richards:[4]

Those who attend the Church Meetings will know that we have recently accepted the resignation of five of our members who are leaving Birmingham, England in order to throw in their lot with the Cotswold Bruderhof at Ashton Keynes in Wiltshire. Among those leaving us is Mr. Guy Johnson who has been a Deacon of Carrs Lane since 1935; and I cannot let the event pass without a word both of regret and goodwill.

Mr. Johnson grew up in the Church, and after absence for University and legal training, returned to us as one of our most devoted and useful

[3]Nancy and her parents moved to the Cotswold Bruderhof in July 1938. Her father, Jabez, died there a month later and was the first adult buried in the little community burial ground. Her mother remained with the community and moved with them to Paraguay. "Mother Watkins" was a favorite person of my dad's.

[4]September 1938 *Carrs Lane Journal*, nos. 5 and 6

members: his election to the Diaconate followed almost inevitably, and as the youngest member of that body, he kept in touch with the more youthful elements in the life and work of the Church. When Mr. Godfrey Pain left us, it was "Guy" who became Leader of the Seventy Club, and it is not too much to say he was — and is — universally loved. His going therefore leaves a gap which it is not easy to fill, and I am one of the many who wish that he had found it possible to remain. But like a growing number of young people today, he feels intensely the injustices of the social-economic order, with its army of unemployed, its inequitable distribution of power and privilege, and its reliance — in many aspects — upon motives and processes which are a flagrant denial of the way of Christ. It is therefore from what he and his associates feel to be the highest demands of Christian loyalty, that they have finally decided to surrender their several callings and throw in their lot with the Cotswold Bruderhof.

My parents, by then engaged to be married, apparently made their formal move to the Cotswold Bruderhof in August 1938, and very soon became novice members. They were both baptized as full members on December 12, 1938, along with twelve other new members, including several from the Seventy Club.

CHAPTER 2 - 1939-1940

The English Cotswolds to Paraguay's Gran Chaco Region

In first visiting the Bruderhof in 1937, I expect my recently engaged parents would surely have been struck by several aspects. First, since most of the members were emigrants from either Germany or Switzerland, the everyday language on the commune was German, not English. German was quite an anomaly in this quiet area of rural Wiltshire, and not surprisingly raised some questions and eyebrows in the neighborhood, especially as the hostilities between Germany and England grew, despite the emigrants' anti-Nazi credentials.

Second, my parents must have wondered about the rather simple middle-European peasant-type clothing of essentially seventeenth- or eighteenth-century vintage worn by most members. This choice reflected the fairly close relationship between the Bruderhof and another communal group, the Hutterites. The Bruderhof, in seeking closer ties with the Hutterites for both religious and perhaps strategic reasons (a future home in North America?), chose to adopt the simple peasant garb that the Hutterites clung to from at least the time of their exodus from eastern Europe. The Hutterites also had maintained their own form of Old German, known as "Hutterisch," rather similar in both origin and construction to Yiddish. The Bruderhof did not adopt this dialect, even as they embraced such rather un-English apparel as polka-dot headscarves for women and very simple trousers for the men with braces (suspenders) rather than belts to hold them up.

Third, gender roles were more clear-cut and old-fashioned than those familiar to Guy and Eleanor. The Hutterites had definite rules, or Ordnungen, on many matters. They also had customs not formally defined by these rules but generally understood in Hutterite and adopted

Eleanor and Guy's wedding procession, Cotswold Bruderhof, January 14, 1939

Eleanor with Guy and their mothers on their wedding day.

"To my Darling Bride in Memory of January 14th 1939"

in Bruderhof settings. For example, as far as I know there was no formal rule about smoking, but women did not smoke, and men tended to avoid it. The Bruderhof recognized that smoking was prohibited within the sect, and adherence to both formal and informal Hutterian rules was an expected, if unwritten, part of the bargain when the Bruderhof began to identify in the 1930s as Hutterian.

Clearly aware of the significant changes life as members of the Bruderhof required, Guy and Eleanor moved into the Cotswold community in August 1938. On January 14, 1939, just over a month after their baptism on December 12, 1938, and two weeks into what would be a dark year for much of Europe, Guy and Eleanor were married at the Cotswold Bruderhof. It was a happy occasion with a lively celebration by the whole community. Though mostly a community event, both my parents' families attended the wedding. In addition to the mothers of both the bride and groom, my dad's brother, David, attended, as did my mother's sister Audrey Ann.

Guy and Eleanor honeymooned for a few days at Morwenstow, a small seaside village in north Cornwall on England's west Atlantic coast. Little could they have foreseen that their next return to Morwenstow would be a full quarter century later, along with several of their children, including their oldest and youngest.

By summer another important event occupied Guy and Eleanor's attention, the imminent arrival of their first child, John Timothy, who was to be known by his middle name, Timothy (or Tim). I arrived at the Cotswold Bruderhof's "mother house" on a gray Sunday afternoon, October 22, 1939, less than two months after Germany's invasion of Poland and

Guy and baby Tim

Britain's declaration two days later of war with Germany.

Even as the population of the little agricultural commune grew past two hundred at Ashton Keynes and overflowed to the nearby village of Oaksey, where Guy and Eleanor lived for a while with their baby, it became clear that their Cotswold Bruderhof was not a permanent home.

Eleanor and baby Tim

Though they were pacifist opponents of Nazism, the Bruderhof members found themselves suddenly redefined by the current political circumstances as "enemy aliens," and under heightened suspicion. There was little open hostility to this curious band of bearded men and peasant-attired women, many speaking only limited English. I do recall Dad telling of a situation where he and a heavily bearded Swiss member, traveling together somewhere in the English Midlands, were overheard conversing in a mix of English and German. They were called in for questioning by the local constabulary, having been reported as possible spies. Though this encounter ended quite amicably, there was increasing hostility to this group, especially in the press and locally. Though central government remained supportive, the commune seriously contemplated emigration of at least part of the community.

Guy and Eleanor, both British, were enthusiastic young members, much engaged in the development of the commune and much aware of the political currents swirling around them, especially the rise of militaristic sentiment reflecting the far more aggressive Nazi Germany. For Guy, as a member of the Bruderhof and of prime military age, this sentiment meant declaring himself a conscientious objector and appearing before a military tribunal in 1940. The tribunal eventually accepted his position and it was covered by the local press under the headline: "Solicitor Who

Evening Advertiser | 30 MAY, 1940

SOLICITOR WHO THREW UP PROFESSION

Joined Bruderhof, Now Granted Exemption

The story of a young law student who became a solicitor and subsequently threw up his profession to become a member of the Bruderhof Brotherhood was told yesterday, at Bristol, when Edward Guy Johnson, bearded and in the rough spun apparel of the Cotswold society, appeared before the South Western Tribunal, and asked for absolute exemption from all forms of military and national service.

Johnson's statement read: "I have held the absolute pacifist position since November, 1934, in which month I wrote to the War Office to the effect that the certificate "A" which I had gained as a boy in the school O.T.C. should be cancelled as in the event of a future war I could not offer myself for military service.

"My pacifist conviction at that time was limited to the simple rejection of war, and I became a member of various peace organisations such as the Fellowship of Reconciliation, the League of Nations Union and the Peace Pledge Union. But all these had little connection with my daily life as a law student and later as a solicitor.

"In the last three years, however, this pacifist conviction has deepened so that now I know that I am called as a follower of Jesus Christ to seek to express the love which He brings in helping to build up a life where not only war but social injustice and greed are entirely overcome in a brotherly way of life, with a common purse, a common table, and a common work together in peace and unity as the friends of this love of Christ.

"In 1938, accordingly, I decided to join the Brothers of the Cotswold Bruderhof, giving up my work as a solicitor. I honour the State, for I recognise law to be a necessity for men who refuse to live in the spirit of love, and I recognise, too, that the State

depends upon the law and that the law depends upon the sanction of force.

"But the way of Christ is altogether different from the way of the State. His call to all men at all times, and His call to me now, is to go His way of absolute love and brotherhood in all circumstances and at whatever cost.

"My request to the tribunal, therefore, is that I be granted unconditional exemption within the meaning of the Act."

Another member of the Brotherhood from the Bruderhof bore testimony to the applicant's sincerity.

Judge Wethered said the tribunal had investigated Bruderhof applications before, and Johnson would be retained on the Conscientious Objectors' Register without condition.

Article in Swindon paper, May 30, 1940

Threw Up Profession," with the subhead "Joined Bruderhof, Now Granted Exemption." The article was dated May 30, 1940, and appeared in the *Evening Advertiser* of Swindon, the nearest sizeable city.

The need was clear for relocation overseas to a site where their dream of a peaceful multinational exercise of their religious calling could be fulfilled. But where would they be welcome?

The New World was seen as a possible haven, with an initial focus on Canada and the United States. After all, these countries had throughout their histories welcomed many religious dissidents, including the Anabaptist groups with whom the Bruderhof communes had affinity, such as the Hutterites. Plans to explore these possibilities proceeded even as the war in Europe and considerable anti-German sentiment grew. The community decided to send two brothers, a Swiss engineer and a British solicitor, to explore possibilities in the New World. Thus it was that on August 1, 1940, Hans Meier and Guy Johnson embarked from Liverpool for New York on the Cunard White Star liner, *Scythia.*

They later recounted these eventful months of exploration, starting with their ocean crossing, during which they were in charge of a young Jewish refugee. They safely delivered him to their prearranged contacts in New York in advance of reuniting him with family who had preceded him out of Europe.

My mother was pregnant with her second child when Dad departed that August. As it unexpectedly turned out, my mother and I would not see my dad again until mid-December of 1940. And not in the United States, but in South America.

A Continental Shift

What changed so drastically after Hans Meier and my dad left for the United States?

In brief, North America in this early WWII period was becoming less welcoming to foreigners seeking to settle there. However, the Bruderhof had established close relations in the United States with some individuals and groups, notably the Mennonites and Hutterites who themselves had earlier emigrated from Europe. They were sympathetic to the Bruderhof

SEPTEMBER 24, 1940

HYDE PARK, Monday–On Saturday I met with a number of people at my apartment in the New York City, who wanted to talk over a variety of things. I think my most unusual visitors were Mr. Hans Meyer and Mr. Guy Johnson. They come from a group who believe in living, here and now, in real brotherhood.

For the moment, while the Government of England understands their position, the people about them are making their community life somewhat difficult, for they have every nationality in the community in order to show that there really is a brotherhood of man. You make no commitment as to any special religion in joining them, you simply are willing to live according to their theories of government.

South Dakota has a similar community, but they are somewhat withdrawn from the other people of the neighborhood. The English group wishes to bring over its members to join those in this country. It is evident that they would be model citizens and their conception of democracy is certainly a pure and practical one. But even these two men with fine, calm faces, agreed that community living was not without its problems. I wonder if it will be easier in South Dakota than in England. I hope so, for they could not fail to be a good influence.

After attending the opening at a department store of designs for household furniture which various American artists had made, I left New York City in a cheerful mood. This work is going to bring taste and beauty to the people in the country because it is within the price range that many can afford. I wish them great success in what is a commercial venture, but at the same time, an artistic one.

Saturday night, to our great joy, James, Elliott and Ruth, and Franklin Jr., and Ethel, were all here for their grandmother's birthday celebration. Our other guests were Mrs. J. R. Roosevelt, Miss Laura Delano, Mr. Langdon P. Marvin, Jr., and Mr. and Mrs. Douglas Fairbanks, Jr. It was a happy family gathering and I hope there will be many more similar ones.

Elliott has decided to go into the Air Corps for the duration of the emergency and his brothers are trying to figure out with his various business commitments, for it is a little disrupting completely to change your life. Today he receives his orders in Washington and will know the exact date when he must report for duty in Dayton, Ohio.

plight and agreed to try to help the group relocate to the United States or Canada. But, as the two brothers soon discovered, isolationist sentiment was growing quickly and made it difficult even among those disposed to help to do so effectively.

Reflecting the political sensitivities of the day, one of Hans and Guy's early meetings was with First Lady Eleanor Roosevelt. She wrote about their conversation in her newspaper column, My Day, on September 24, 1940. They also met with government officials and others to explain their situation and explore possible approaches to facilitate the hoped-for emigration. Welcome as such support was, the main effort was through contacts with their Anabaptist cousins, the Hutterites and Mennonites, notably Orie Miller, who at that time headed the Mennonite Central Committee (MCC). Although Dad did visit a couple of the South Dakota Hutterite colonies to explore that area, their main focus was on the northeastern United States and eastern Canada, where they met with government officials and groups such as the MCC.

As the situation in Europe grew more dire, the already uncertain opportunities in the United States and Canada were evaporating. This information was relayed to the Cotswold Bruderhof in England. It became clear that a Bruderhof exodus to North America would not be forthcoming soon enough, so alternatives needed to be explored. At this point, the MCC, spearheaded by Miller, became instrumental in opening the door to a new possibility: Paraguay, in South America! (I can imagine the questions at the Cotswold Bruderhof, mostly in German, *"Woh ist das denn?"* In English, "Where is that?").

The Mennonites had established a settlement about ten years earlier in the deep interior of Paraguay, known as the Gran Chaco, and some years later had started another in a more hospitable, yet still rather isolated, part of the country.

In a leap of faith and with few choices, the decision was made to close down the Cotswold Bruderhof and move the entire group of over three hundred people to Paraguay.

The British Home Office was involved in the next phase of selling and closing the Cotswold Bruderhof and facilitating travel to Paraguay for this large contingent at a time when transatlantic crossings were already dangerous due to lurking German submarines.

The main exodus from the Cotswold Bruderhof to Paraguay began with eighty-one passengers, including my pregnant mother, Eleanor, and me as a thirteen-month-old baby. The *Andalucia Star* departed Liverpool on November 24, 1940 for South America, headed for the uncertainties of life on a new continent. The exodus spanned several more voyages, mostly during the first half of 1941. To avoid enemy submarines, the ships took circuitous routes. The passengers were kept in the dark, but my mother was delighted to recognize the iconic sharp-edged profile of the Cuillin mountains on the Isle of Skye, where she and friends from Carrs Lane church had enjoyed a hiking holiday, as the *Andalucia Star* steamed past. It is sobering to reflect that none of the ships carrying the successive early 1941 Bruderhof groups across the Atlantic survived the war (the *Andalucia Star* was sunk by a U-boat in October 1942).

Both vessels, the one carrying my dad from America, USS *Uruguay*, and the one carrying my mother and me, *Andalucia Star,* docked in Rio de Janeiro, Brazil, on December 12. Guy was able to hire a small harbor boat to take him to the *Andalucia Star* but his travel documents did not permit him to transfer. Their long-awaited reunion required a few more days until a few days until we all landed in Buenos Aires, Argentina, on December 18.

One of my earliest memories dates to that time in December 1940 and this reunion. Who was the bearded stranger who suddenly occupied so much of my mother's attention? Fortunately, I quickly warmed to him, "my daddy!"

Gran Chaco

The whole contingent of new arrivals departed Buenos Aires by a shallow-draft river steamer on December 21,

Guy, 1940

churning up the mighty Rio Parana and arriving at Paraguay's capital, Asunción, on Christmas Day, 1940. There, they transferred to a canvas-roofed barge, on which they did their best to celebrate the date in the heat of the tropical summer in their new land. Not easy, when Christmas candles melted in the unrelenting heat of summer!

As evening fell two days later, the barge was towed upriver against

strong currents. After the long, slow voyage of 190 miles, and several local stops, they arrived at the tiny river port of Puerto Casado/Puerto Esperanza. They disembarked on December 30 for the final overland stages of their odyssey from Puerto Casado to the main Mennonite colony, Filadelfia, their temporary new home in Chaco.

From Puerto Casado, a narrow-gauge rail line headed farther into the rough and arid terrain of the Gran Chaco. The weary pioneers took it as far as it went to a junction known as Kilometer 145. I know from my parents and others of the significant challenges of those last two overland travel days. Due to some communication

Woodcut of oxen wagon trains
by Leslie Holland, a family friend

snags with Filadelfia, they were stuck temporarily with little shelter and sustenance at Kilometer 145 until several young Mennonite carters arrived with ox wagons, and in the relative cool of the evening, headed out on New Year's Eve toward their destination. They stopped around midnight, then on New Year's morning, January 1, 1941, resumed their wagon trek with only a break for a few hours during the midday and midsummer heat of the Tropic of Capricorn, so unlike the cool climate and seasons they'd left behind in England.

After a brief nighttime stop, the wagon train continued very early Friday morning, January 2, with arrival in Filadelfia later that morning. There, their Mennonite hosts made them very welcome, preparing and offering a good breakfast — their first real meal in some days!

Eleanor with Tim and others, Chaco, February 1941

I remember very little of this or the next three months in Chaco or our travels out of Chaco in March. Yet vague memories persist from those travels. Memories of being very hungry, and of being given hard little bread balls, known locally as "galletas," to chew on. No such luxuries as butter or jam, of course, but those galletas did stay the pangs of hunger!

Seven Johnson siblings visiting the former school and our first home in
Filadelfia, Gran Chaco, Paraguay, 2005

The physical layout of Filadelfia was dominated by a schoolhouse built by
the settlers. They generously made most of it available to their temporary
guests, where the majority of the approximately eighty guests lived dorm
style on the lower floor while becoming acquainted both with their hosts
and with the physical challenges of life in this new environment.

CHAPTER 3 - 1941-1947

Primavera Bruderhofs, Paraguay

Within the first week of our arrival to the Chaco, the Bruderhof numbers were augmented by two babies, Jan-Peter Fros and Emily Paul. A third arrived a month later on February 4, 1941, my sister Joy Barbara, whose name reflected both the hope and the joy she represented and the foreignness of this New World her parents brought her into. The fourth, and final, "Chaco baby," Lydia, was born to Margaret and Hans Meier on March 12. By then a new and more permanent home outside the Chaco was well into the planning stages for the entire community and not just the initial eighty-three Chaco pioneers.

Eleanor and Tim with baby Joy, July 1941

Soon however, the limited prospects for settlement in the sparsely populated and geographically isolated Chaco led to a search for a more promising site for a viable, self-sufficient community able to accommodate the main contingent from England that was coming in several transatlantic batches. By the end of March, almost all the original contingent, though deeply grateful to their Chaco hosts, had left for a new site. It was near the second established Mennonite colony, named Friesland in memory of their Dutch origins, and located on the East side of the Paraguay river in the more centrally located San Pedro region. This new Bruderhof site would be named Primavera.

After the heat, aridity, and thorny scrub forest of the Chaco, the lush vegetation of the newly selected site about twenty miles east of Puerto Rosario, was a welcome change when we and the other "Chaco pioneers" arrived in March 1941.

In February, the Bruderhof agreed to purchase a large estate from its owner, named Rutenberg. It was an estancia of 8,000-plus hectares (21,000 acres) of mixed campos (open land for cattle ranching and agriculture) and jungle. Almost immediately after purchase, the work work of establishing the first commune commenced at a site named Isla Margarita.

Letter from Eberhard (Hardi) Arnold and Guy Johnson to the Bruderhof communities asking for specific support as they created the Isla Margarita commune, February 1941

Filadelfia,
Fernheim,
Puerto Casado,
Chaco, Paraguay.

February 1941.

Dear Friend,

Very many of the friends whom our brothers Hans Meier and Guy Johnson met during their journeyings last autumn in the United States and Canada have asked that we, the members of the Society of Brothers, keep in touch with them and let them know when we arrive in Paraguay, what adventures befall us there and how we are getting on.

So we are writing this this open letter to you, and it is our sincere hope this this will only be the beginning of a long and ever deepening contact with you all.

After a voyage of 24 days, during which the danger of bombs, mines and submarine raiders was added to the usual perils and discomforts of the Atlantic in mid-winter, our ship, the Andalucia Star, sailed into Buenos Aires on 17th December, with 81 of us on board. We all feel deeply thankful to God for his wonderful protection at this time, especially as our pioneer group includes 40 small children, 12 of whom are babies.

At Buenos Aires we boarded the 'Ciudad de Corrientes', the little river steamer that was to take us up the Rio Parana into Paraguay. It was here, on our long river trip, that we first began to realise what 'change of climate' really means, and our bewildered northern European bodies received a fierce shock. Moreover it became very clear to us what a colossal distinction there is in South America between 1st class and 3rd class, between rich and poor, and how it is true in all lands that the poor are treated the worst and suffer the most. It was nothing less than a miracle that the health and strength of us all was preserved during these 10 days on the Rio Parana, and, further inland, on the Rio Paraguay. The conditions, especially sleeping accomodation, were bad beyond anything we had expected.

On 25th December we found ourselves at Asuncion, the capital of Paraguay; it was blazing hot (104 in the shade) and not easy for us to experience that it was in fact Christmas Day, for it is midsummer now in Paraguay. We were now moved from our steamer to a small barge, which was attached by ropes to another boat and after 2 days waiting we proceeded up the river side by side. Living conditions became now even more primitive, and the only compensation was the excitement, especially of the children, upon catching sight of real live crocodiles, storks and beautiful parrots, along the green banks of the Rio Paraguay. But the mosquitos that plagued us by night became less and less a novelty and more and more a nuisance.

At long last we arrived in Puerto Casado, a tiny riverside port lying just north of the tropic of Capricorn. Here we spent a memorable night encamped on the river bank, accompanied by innumerable insects. The following morning we caught the one

- 3 -

accumulated, so that there has already been a tremendous amount of work for our doctor. He has far more to do than he can possibly tackle and it will be a relief when our other two doctors, who travel with the next big group, arrive to work by his side.

One super difficulty that we have yet to overcome is that transport is so bad, and functions - when it functions at all - so weakly here in the heart of South America, that all news, information and correspondence reaches us only after long delay. A cable, for example, from England or the U.S. can easily take anything from two to three weeks to reach us, and letters require a proportionately longer time. Yet we do know that 3 more brothers have already arrived by cargo boat in Buenos Aires' and should soon be with us; also that the next big group of brothers, sisters and children hope to leave for South America before the end of February. But of course the shipping position is extremely serious and there is never any certainty as regards sailing dates.

In spite of all the hardships and difficulties however - and especially the sickness which has begun such a subtil and insidious attack, it has become absolutely clear to us that God wills to unite us all in this land - somewhere - that we, together with all others who feel called to join us, may carry on, at all costs, an uncompromising witness for real peace, brotherly love, and economic and social justice.

So ever since we arrived we have been sending out brothers in groups, North, South, East and West, to seek out a place where we can settle 350 people immediately and which will allow for limitless expansion. The search has not yet ended, but we have faith that the place where we are to build up will be shown to us.

In the meantime we can report with joy that not only our witness for medical work but also our witness for full community have been received with thankfulness by many people here. We have found many open hearts and enthusiastic seeking for a new way of life.

When we have found a home, when our people have all arrived from England (with the exception of a few remaining for mission work there) and when our new Bruderhof Community has been started and established we plan to have, once again, a printing shop so that we may be able to send books, as well as letters, to all our friends, wherever they may be. For the present, however, we know that you will understand that in this pioneer stage of our venture it is not possible to write as fully as we would like.

We have to close with an S.O.S. Owing to the wartime restrictions on the export of capital and other machinery from England on the export of agricultural and other machinery from England we stand in urgent need of help. Because this is a strange land and prices are still new to us it is at the moment not possible to give full details, nor can we tell you the exact total which we must find. But it is clear that the following are needed at once and some American dollars would be a very great help towards obtaining them :-

However, when my parents and the other Bruderhofers arrived in March to Primavera, they lacked real shelter until they were able to build simple structures like the rudimentary mud-floored, thatched-roof hall where my parents and their two youngsters (new baby Joy and I) lived with several other families.

The rest of the Cotswold group began to arrive shortly thereafter, with the largest contingent of 160 arriving in April just a few weeks after our "Chaco pioneer" group arrived. Soon, all 334 Bruderhofers (adults and children) from England had arrived and needed to be accommodated, partly at the Mennonite colony of Friesland. Primitive structures were built at Isla

-4-

1. Plows, harrows, seed drills, hoes, spades and all kinds of agricultural machines, tools and equipment.

2. Horses, mules and oxen.

3. Wagons (until we are in a position to build our own).

4. Truck.

5. Tractor.

6. Wood-gas engine for power.

7. Large water pump and other machinery.

8. Fruit trees: we need to plant trees immediately so that the community may in 2-4 years have fruit.

9. Cattle and general livestock. The pasture here is relatively poorer on the average than in England or U.S.A. so that the milk yield is less and the number of cows needed proportionately greater. A herd of 300 milking cows is estimated.

10. Sawmill equipment (essential for building).

11. Hospital equipment and supplies. Especially: operating table, X-ray plant, kerosene, Protargol, Thymol. This is the most urgent need of all, not only for our community but for the entire neighbourhood.

This is by no means a complete or detailed schedule but does include our most urgent needs. And the last one mentioned is the most important of all - equipment and medical supplies for a hospital.

Do please help. Funds can be posted or cabled to - c/o Hans Meier, Banco de Londres y America del Sud, Asuncion, Paraguay. (Cable address: Londonbank, Asuncion).

The whole Brotherhood joins in sending a warm greeting, in the strong hope that more and more men and women will, in this time of war, be drawn together everywhere in common seeking and striving for the new and coming order of active peace, brotherly justice and real unity..

Yours in friendship,
for THE SOCIETY OF BROTHERS.

Eberhard C.H. Arnold.

(PS in Guy Johnson's handwriting)

PS. Since the typing of this letter two items of very joyful news have come in
1) We have found land where we can immediately begin to build up anew. The address is Primavera, Alto Paraguay. S. America.

2) We have learnt by cable from Rio that 158 of our people, including 12 children, have been brought in safety across the Atlantic & arrived at Buenos Aires on 1st March. That is really wonderful news & fills us with thanksgiving. At the same time & clearly give added urgency to the Pioneer task before us.

Guy's PS

Johnsons and other Primavera pioneers, July 1941

Margarita as rapidly as possible, and most of us were crowded temporarily into three *hallen* (halls or longhouses). Flimsy curtains provided the only vestige of family privacy between compartments, supplemented by some of the luggage crates in which family belongings had been transported.

Constructing the first buildings in the Primavera commune was an on-the-job learning experience and some of the early lessons were painful. The story passed down was that these European pilgrims, based on their European experience, started their first building from its mud walls upward, expecting to put the thatch roof on last. Sadly, before the walls went up, heavy seasonal rains pelted down. Mournful Bruderhofers watched in dismay as yet-unhardened walls dissolved into their original mud. I'm told that I, a toddler in my mother's arms, seeing these crestfallen adults, piped up and said, "Never mind, Mummy. I'll mend it with a piece of string." Apparently, my innocent remark brought some chuckles and light relief to my dispirited adult companions. Future construction benefited greatly from the advice of local folks.

Though they made many mistakes in the application of their European building and agrarian skills in this very different geography, the "brothers and sisters," by dint of hard work and a strong spirit of cooperation, soon began to make real progress in improving their housing, developing schools and kindergartens for their many youngsters, planting gardens for both familiar and unfamiliar crops, and in managing the free-range cattle scattered over the estancia. They also established brickworks with a large kiln as well as a sawmill, which aided the ongoing construction work using timber from their extensive forests.

It is a tribute to the resourcefulness of the Bruderhof refugees that they survived the first year as well as they did — largely thanks to the Mennonite settlers who helped them with shelter and food. By the second year, the Bruderhofers had established a solid base for expanding beyond their initial village of Isla Margarita.

Health Realities

Dealing with health challenges was more problematic, and almost all participants suffered from various tropical ailments. The first death of a young child occurred in March 1941, and several more died within the next year. Morbidity was rampant, especially from various infections, including severe and temporarily blinding conjunctivitis (initially misdiagnosed as trachoma), and from acute and chronic gastrointestinal ailments, malaria, and a variety of other tropical and heat-related problems, particularly in the first two to three years.

Some of the childhood ailments we experienced were a combination of the usual childhood infections and other ailments common also to Europe at that time. Others were more typical of our new environment and impoverished conditions. Our footwear, when we had any, was mainly a sort of sandal with leather straps over a wooden sole. We used the German term *klepper* for these. More often, we went barefoot which, quite commonly, resulted in sand flea infestations, which required rather painful efforts to extract the eggs and larvae with needles from the soles of our feet.

Small-insect infestations of our hair (presumably lice) were sometimes treated with DDT powder, rubbed into our scalps. Today, that would not be the treatment of choice, but choices were very constrained for us!

I was unlucky enough at an early age (maybe three or four) to require quarantining when I contracted a nasty case of tropical conjunctivitis, which sealed my eyes for several days. Thankfully, the initial diagnosis of trachoma turned out to be wrong.

I spent my quarantine in a small and rather dark hut close to the little hospital the commune was establishing. Oddly, the sight that greeted me when my eyes opened enough to see was of a lad (teenager, I believe) sitting outside the hut, occupying himself by skinning a fairly large snake. Not really a sight for sore eyes! A number of the young men collected snake skins, many of them quite colorful, and decorated their walls with these mementos. I suspect that in the understandable desire to rid the area of snakes around our buildings, little effort was made to ensure that only poisonous snakes were killed.

Loma Hoby

In early 1942, the second colony or *hof* was established less than two miles from Isla Margarita on the low hill on which the former owner of the Primavera estancia had built his home. This was Loma Hoby, meaning "blue hill" in Guarani, and here quite soon the Bruderhof began to build a little hospital to serve the needs not only of the Bruderhof communities, but also of the badly underserved local population. Our family moved from Isla Margarita to Loma Hoby early in 1943, first to a site very near the newly established hospital, and later a little farther away next to the "school wood" where the new school was being built. Our home overlooked the campo and the line of forest beyond the campo.

I remember this view as being very much surrounded by nature and especially lovely when lapacho trees were in bloom.

We shared this little thatched cottage with shuttered windows with the Lloyd and Joy Jones family. Our half was basically one good-sized mud-floored room with a little alcove. It was just a short walk to the outdoor lavatory. There was, of course, no running water. The nearby well provided buckets of water Dad or others would bring to our washbasin in the alcove.

In the next two years, our little Johnson family expanded considerably, first with Barnabas's arrival on May 8, 1943, and then Susan on September

View of blooming lapacho trees, painted by Primavera resident Clementina Jaime

16, 1944. I have only indistinct and slightly confused memories of those two events, though I was already aware that quite often one family or another would be visited by "angels" (not storks!) and a new arrival would be welcomed, often with singing to the mother and new baby at the mother house, where the new baby would be held up for all to see and welcomed into the commune.

A day or two later, mother and baby would return home. She would be given about six weeks of postpartum freedom from usual work routines as she bonded with the arrival.

So it was for Joy and me on these two occasions. Our family routine was interrupted for a day or two as other adults looked after us, after which suddenly we'd be told that the angels had brought us a new baby brother, Barnabas, and then later another sister, Susan. Joy and I would be taken by Dad to the mother house to see the new arrival and our mother, a happy occasion if still rather puzzling to this youngster!

Births were recognized as important events, and birth anniversaries were acknowledged with simple but happy celebrations of birthdays by family and by peers. As for most Bruderhof occasions, group singing played a big part along with cake and usually candles. The child whose birthday was being celebrated often received one or two simple gifts.

My fifth birthday was about a month after my sister Susan's birth and was the first birthday I really remember, thanks to my delight at an unexpected homemade gift. This future pacifist was surprised and pleased to receive a "dagger," though in actuality it was a rather blunt metal blade embedded into a wooden handle. It was more useful as a digging than a cutting tool yet seemed such a grown-up gift to a five-year-old. Did it ever occur to me to use it against a living creature? Not sure what I thought, but it was a "big boy's" thing, so gratefully accepted! Did I think of that old dagger when I picked up a real sword and scabbard, more than two decades later, during a trip to Afghanistan? It also never violated my basically pacifist instincts, nor was it intended to. Yet, I could hardly fail to wonder what its earlier history may have been, given where I acquired it.

Schooling

From the infants' baby house, one generally progressed with one's age-mates through the various children's departments. The names reflected the predominant Germanic influence: the crawling toddlers would be in the *Krabbelhaus*, from which they progressed to *Kindergarten*, followed by preschool, typically with a different set of adults minding each group of young charges.

This was the age when we not only began more serious exploration of the natural world around us but also were increasingly socialized into our Bruderhof culture through singing, group games, stories (mostly traditional German and with little actual relevance to our daily lives in Paraguay), and the beginnings of exposure to reading and writing.

After preschool, one progressed to *Schule* with this major transition marked by the important ceremony of Einschulung, with students, parents, teachers, and others in attendance. It was during my *Einschulung* that I acquired a nickname. Our commune age groups were somewhat bilingual, but we usually spoke mostly German.

In preschool I'd learned the basics of the alphabet and a few simple words, such as my name, T-I-M, to demonstrate my readiness for *schule*.

The little ceremony was held outdoors in the school wood and we demonstrated our newly learned skills. Since another youngster occupied the left side of the blackboard, I started from the right side, to which I was not

Kindergarten, October 1942

accustomed. No problem: starting from the right I carefully wrote the letters of my name. Laughter from the adults, and flustered shame from me, though I wasn't sure what I'd done amiss. I'd spelled out correctly T-I-M but starting at the right margin. To them, it was M-I-T! To a few people, Mit henceforth became my nickname. Not too bad, really, when one considers that the German word for "with" is *mit*. Better certainly than its opposite, *ohne*, meaning "without"!

I started my first grade of primary school in a class of first and second graders in one of the small buildings in the school wood. Instruction by different teachers (mostly women at that time) was mainly in German. My memories from that age are rather vague, but I do remember that our more formal schoolwork included reading and writing in German and English (depending perhaps on who the instructor was), along with something fairly new to me, arithmetic, to which I took very readily, unlike some of my classmates. Playtimes and group games and singing continued to be major components of our education, as was the absorption of the natural world surrounding us.

Near the start of our last year in Paraguay, on April 19, 1947, my parents' third daughter and fifth child, Elizabeth, was born. Shortly afterward, in May, our family moved from Loma Hoby to the new and barely established third Primavera community, named Ibatè. Ibatè was still a tiny settlement, with only a few thatched-roof with mud-walled buildings. We occupied part of one of these, and my mother became the teacher to the small number of first to third graders in these families. Our school was mainly our family living room, with new baby Elizabeth behind a screen in a corner of the same room.

For us younger pupils, much of our school day was spent in outdoor activities such as walks in the surrounding forest and fields, learning of nature by immersion in it and with the guidance of more knowledgeable adults. Meanwhile a couple of slightly older (preteen) children made a daily trek, usually on foot along the dried-mud paths through open fields and woodlands, to Isla Margarita's much larger school less than two miles away.

Nature

Growing up, the rhythms of nature were our constant companion. At night, the absence of artificial lighting beyond dim kerosene lamps gave us wonderful views of the heavens. Brilliant stars and constellations, the broad sky-river of the Milky Way, the moon and its phases — all explained to us, mainly by Dad. Mother, a teacher by training and instinct, introduced us and other children to the way the sun seemed to travel across the heavens. I remember her instructing us to trace the path of the shadow of a stick she stuck in the sand, explaining how this movement related to the sun above us. Because we lived on the Tropic of Capricorn, in December (the Southern Hemisphere's summer) the sun was directly overhead. As midday approached, the shadow would disappear, only to reappear a bit later on the other side!

And marvel of marvels, we witnessed a near-total solar eclipse in early 1947. Dad had some smoked glass and other devices to protect our eyes for the occasion. As he took the older children out to watch, the sun began to disappear. Toward the maximum totality, the air grew distinctly cooler, nature's sounds shifted, and day birds' chatter gave way to the mournful sounds of other species evening songs. Soon, the sun came back with its warmth and bird life, but I confess to being worried, for a while! Now I understand how awestruck our ancestors over the millennia were by these sorts of celestial phenomena. Even in this century, I find in myself some of that primal wonder, though not the fear of ancient times. In later years, I've found my way to total solar eclipses viewed from Mexico, France, and two from the United States.

Our immersion in nature included mostly enjoyable walks during which we learned about some of the plants and animals along our paths. Among animals, some of the more interesting were the occasional troops of monkeys moving in the forest canopy above us. These were mostly quite small, and also not noisy, unlike the booming howler monkeys we would sometimes hear at some distance but see less frequently.

The richness and diversity of the South American bird species that surrounded us was something I did not fully appreciate until much later when we'd left to return to Europe. Familiar sights included the varieties of colorful and often noisy parrots. Weaver birds with their communities of nests hanging from tree branches fascinated me, but so did the toucans, with their enormous colored beaks. Overhead, vultures (German name *aasgeier*) would circle on the rising thermals that developed as the sun rose, indicating the likely location of the next meal these carrion scavengers were anticipating. In contrast to the large, slowly circling vultures were the colorful little fast-moving hummingbirds (colibris) flitting from blossom to blossom in search of nectar. I recall the wonderment of first seeing a tiny and very neatly built hummingbird nest, well camouflaged along a pathway near the jungle.

Sometimes we'd see several large birds running across the open campos. We called the birds "ostriches" (German name *Strauss*) but they were in fact the smaller version of these African savanna birds, the South American rhea. Nearly sixty years later, in 2005, during a nostalgic visit to my childhood home, I was told that with forest decimation and other human encroachment I was unlikely to see any of these flightless but fast-running pampas birds. I was therefore delighted when one turned up as we visited the site of the former Bruderhof graveyard. Unfortunately, it was only one, not a group, but nonetheless a memory of yesteryear.

Paraguayan insects and arthropods were also remarkable in their variety, including the hundreds of colorful butterflies by day, fireflies at night, lots of different beetles and stick-insect specimens, as well as various types of grasshoppers and spiders. All these were interesting to a young lad, including some creatures one generally avoided such as tarantulas, scorpions, and hornets, which could cause hours of misery if one had the misfortune of a direct encounter. Fortunately, they also generally preferred to avoid us.

Reptiles and amphibians were a constant presence, and mostly both interesting and harmless to us. One memorable encounter made quite an impression on me, and apparently on someone else, who reminded me of it many years later and on a different continent.

Though the event occurred in Paraguay when I was about six, I'll start the story about forty years later in England, where verification came through an unexpected but pleasant meeting.

My wife and I were on a visit to relatives, including my aunt and uncle in East Sussex, where they were still living at the successor commune to the one I'd left decades earlier. We were shown around to see how the commune now operated. I was introduced to a couple of people who were new to me, but then to an older man with a familiar name from a bygone day. When Walter H. heard my name, his eyes lit up. *"Ach, Timmy, errinerst du dich noch an die Klapperschlange?"* ("Tim, do you still remember the rattlesnake?")

It was now my turn to light up, and to call my wife to join the conversation, for here was someone who could corroborate a vivid childhood memory I'd told her about.

Here's the story: It was about midday, and I was at home alone for my siesta. My siblings were elsewhere with their age groups, and my parents were at the communal dining room having lunch. Our home was very primitive, with mud floors and walls and a thatched roof. Not surprisingly, various little creatures found their way inside our home. A few were somewhat welcome, including the large toads that would hop in and reduce the population of mosquitoes and other unwelcome insects.

Our windows had shutters but no glass, so from my little bed I was entertained by looking out at such things as wild guinea pigs and a variety of chattering parrots and other birds. But this time, it was an unusual commotion on the inside that caught my attention. Moving unusually fast, a large toad hopped out from under my parents' bed and in my general direction. Right behind it, and moving even faster, was a large snake. I'd seen plenty of snakes, including some really big ones such as boa constrictors, but not in our home! I didn't hesitate, nor try to reach the door, but jumped out of the window, and ran as fast as I could toward the dining room. Yes, I was running scared!

Lunch was ending, and I blurted my story to the first adults I saw. I'm sure my terror was obvious, and several came back along the path to our home, with Walter picking up a large stick along the way. He opened our door carefully, not knowing quite what he'd find, nor where the snake might be. I was close, though not too close, behind him. It was an ugly sight! The toad had not gotten much further than when I'd escaped through the window, and the snake must have struck. Now, it was curled against the foot of my baby sister Susan's crib, with the toad already well down its gullet, and with blood all around.

Having partially consumed its prey, the snake could not quickly release it in order to escape. Walter's cudgel quickly finished it off, though it took a while for its writhing to stop. He then took it, along with what remained of the unfortunate toad, to a quick cremation in the open fire near our dining room.

I'd understandably not taken time to identify the snake's species, but the large, segmented rattle told us this was indeed a *klapperschlange*, jogging Walter's and my memories so many years later!

Despite such dramatics as the occasional *klapperschlange* type of encounter, we generally lived in a sort of "live and let live" harmony with nature. I think most Bruderhofers tried not to dwell on those parts of our environment that included mosquitoes, locusts, hornets, sand fleas, and a host of other negatives, except to the extent they could not be avoided. I know my own memories tend to the pleasanter images of my childhood. Building a viable community in this non-European environment was a struggle, especially for the adults, including my parents. I'm grateful still to those pioneers, who helped us to concentrate on growing up in a world where my memories are more of butterflies, lizards, guinea pigs, and climbing trees than on those hardships!

Loma Hospital

The Loma hospital was built and developed as a much-needed resource beyond just the Bruderhof, to include Primavera's Mennonite neighbors and the indigenous local populace. The hospital and associated health activities eventually became a major focus of Primavera, welcomed by most not only as an integral component of their community and its development, but also as an expression of their Christian values. That was certainly true when we were there, and for some years beyond when the hospital reportedly served up to sixty thousand people in the hinterland.

To maintain the hospital and the expansion of its staff and activities was expensive. From the start, these needs led to a search for external financial support both locally and in Europe through the new Wheathill Bruderhof, and later, increasingly in North America.

These efforts eventually engendered some backlash and exposed latent divisions, which rocked the Bruderhof to its core about twenty years after Primavera's founding. The larger schism within the Bruderhof movement was between those who felt there was too much emphasis on supporting the work of the hospital, which detracted from the founding generation's emphasis on a religious and communitarian mission to the world, and those who felt this effort was actually an expression of that original mission. Support for the hospital-related work became an unfortunate victim, in the eyes of many, in the abandonment of Primavera and the expulsion of many, many members in the early 1960s.

Communication with the Outside World

Communication during WWII between Europe and rural Paraguay was difficult but gradually improved in the postwar period. At some point, a schedule for periodic radio-telephone contact was established with the small, rotating Bruderhof staff in the capital city, who facilitated communication with the outside world. I recall how puzzled I was the first time I saw this in operation with my dad. A box with voices coming out of it, including the familiar voice of someone I knew was far away, over the horizon, in Asunción! Dad then gave me an introduction to the wonders of modern telecommunications.

Travel among the three Primavera villages was mostly on foot, on horseback, or by ox wagon. A few years later, the commune acquired a "lorry" (a truck) which considerably reduced the time required to go between our villages and the port of Rosario on the Rio Paraguay, from which one could catch an overnight boat downriver to the capital. In the occasional dire medical emergency that could not be handled by the community's own little hospital and medical staff, the radiophone would be used to arrange for a small single-engine plane to come in for a bumpy open field landing to pick up the patient.

Civil Conflict

Major international wars between Paraguay and its neighboring countries, which decimated Paraguay's population, preceded the Bruderhof's arrival. However, after our arrival, civil conflicts periodically erupted. Despite the Bruderhof's efforts to avoid involvement in such political conflicts, inevitably some did affect the communities. National partisan combatants really did not understand the political pacifism of the group, but in general took no direct action against members, beyond such things as commandeering some of our horses or stealing various items. Occasionally clouds of dust in the distance would alert us that soldiers were close by. Only once do I recall some of us youngsters hiding in the jungle adjoining the Isla–Loma "road" (dirt track), while they passed on the dusty path. We were instructed by our minders to remain very silent and not move, and I still recall the sense of fear and foreboding. Were we really in any danger from them? We didn't choose to find out, but the anxious memory remains.

On another occasion it was a couple of military jeeps that came by, on a more official mission. I had no real concept of military or political leaders but somehow found myself among a few youngsters who were asked to sing some sort of Bruderhof song (presumably in German) to these military-garbed and armed men who spoke neither German nor English. Only later did I learn that the main person in this contingent was the military leader, President Higinio Morinigo.

Return to England

Once World War II ended, international travel to and from Paraguay picked up. Such travel was sometimes to aid mission outreach activities but also served to facilitate beneficial personnel exchanges to place members with particular skills where they were most needed. Sometimes the exchanges were to return European members in Paraguay back to Europe, especially those with skills to address the needs of the reestablished Bruderhof at Wheathill. As a young child, I was not privy to the decision-making process, but a collective Primavera decision was made in 1947 that our family would return to England.

Thus it was that in November, our family, now including five young children, headed for Asunción, the beginning of our trip back to England. We left Ibatè by truck on November 5 for our little river port of Rosario on the Rio Paraguay. The little passenger boat, Pingo, took us downriver overnight to Asunción, our home for our final three weeks in Paraguay.

Asunción was a revelation. As we were transported from the river-boat to our Bruderhof temporary home, I saw, with wide-eyed amazement, sights I'd never imagined — buildings galore, far grander than anything I'd seen before, cars and trolleys and a locomotive, so large, noisy, and frightening compared to our placid ox-drawn wagons!

Our main stop was the British consulate, where Dad took us to get our travel documents in order. Prominently displayed was a portrait of a distinguished but unfamiliar gentleman. My innocent question to my dad, "Who is that man?" embarrassed him, but seemed to amuse the consular officer. "That is your king!" It was a portrait of George VI. I'm not sure I'd ever quite grasped the concept of the British monarchy (though aware of fairy-tale kings and queens) from our egalitarian and backwoods international commune. Many more lessons on this new world surely lay ahead for my siblings and me!

Toward the end of November, we boarded the substantially larger shallow-draft river steamer, *Corrientes*, for the three-day voyage down the mighty Rio Parana to Buenos Aires, Argentina. In retrospect, I suppose what we experienced was not unlike the early Mississippi River travelers on those rather shallow-draft vessels described by Mark Twain's accounts. Unfortunately, it would be some years before I would enjoy Twain's descriptions, but I do recall passengers fishing with their feet hanging over the edge of the boat as we worked our way downriver. In one unscheduled delay, our steamer was briefly caught on a sandbar. But soon enough, we found ourselves in the ever-widening estuary of the Parana Rio Plata system headed into Buenos Aires and being taken to our hosts, the Kobrak family. More wonders of modern life were revealed there, including fizzy

drinks, flush toilets, moving stairways, and the shocking inadvisability of sticking my finger into an electric light socket!

With further arrangements for our ocean voyage completed, within a week we were ready to embark on MV *Highland Brigade* headed for England. There would be several stops on the way as the ship, though in part designed as a passenger vessel, was principally a cargo vessel.

On December 5 we began the three-week voyage. The trip included stops to pick up freight in Montevideo, Santos, Rio de Janeiro, Las Palmas, Lisbon, and finally Vigo, before heading through a North Atlantic storm in the Bay of Biscay on Christmas Eve and Day, 1947.

Of this storm, I have two main memories. First, of a massive wave sweeping across the decks and into the ship's dining room, where the crew was gamely trying to set up a festive Christmas dinner for the few passengers who ventured from their cabins. Between the listing ship and the sluicing water, our Christmas dinner ended up on the floor!

Second, my younger brother, Barnabas, and I shared our little two-bunk cabin with two senior Servants of the Word, Hans Zumpe and Balz Trümpi, who were also traveling to Wheathill. Nothing serves as a better leveler of status, I think, than the shared misery of heaving ships and heaving stomachs. Though Hans and Balz probably did a better job of maintaining their dignity than Barnabas and I did, I think the experience gave the lie to the notion that "misery loves company." However, the shared experience was also one that forever gave me a warmer, more human feeling for these two men than I think many younger Bruderhofers had. To me they were, henceforth, mainly the daddies of children they'd temporarily left behind in Paraguay and greatly missed, not just the aloof authority figures some understandably feared.

I cannot help but wonder what my parents' reactions must have been, both spoken and unspoken, as they bade farewell to their Primavera home and communal companions, their "brothers and sisters" in Paraguay. At the time we left Primavera, the three communities had grown, mainly by natural increase of many more births than deaths, to about five hundred people from the approximately three hundred forty people who arrived by early June, 1941.

My parents headed for the home country they'd left a little more than seven years earlier and where now a new community, Wheathill, offspring of the abandoned Cotswold venture, awaited them in a country still emerging from the ghastly conflict of WWII. Surely, their reactions were mixed. Among other things, they had left with one child but were returning with five!

My guess is that a thankfulness for their safe return, with five reasonably healthy children, and a hopefulness for what the future might hold outweighed their regrets in leaving those with whom they'd shared these intense years of building Primavera into a thriving venture, now far advanced from the difficult circumstances under which it had been launched.

The Johnson family, December 1947

The Johnsons aboard the MV Highland Brigade

CHAPTER 4 - 1947-1955

The Wheathill Bruderhof, Shropshire, England

December 27, 1947 - England!

One of the sacrifices members made when joining the Bruderhof was leaving close relationships with their immediate families who were outside the community. Their religious vows made explicit the primacy of their relationship to the Bruderhof church community beyond any other relationship, including even spouses and children. In our case, this distancing was greatly exacerbated during the Paraguay years by the physical distance, plus obstacles to communication, resulting from the war. This sacrifice of the relationship with their parents and siblings must have been very difficult for Guy and Eleanor, yet it was a choice they made.

I can hardly imagine what their parents must have felt, not having themselves made the decision to sever ties, yet suffering from the consequences of the decision. My mother's brother, Tom, told us years later, after we had left the Bruderhof, that when my mother, with me aged one, visited her Cheshire family for a farewell visit before embarking for Paraguay, he found their father sitting alone on a bale of hay in an outhouse, weeping. The families knew, at least to the extent that infrequent letters could tell them, of the significant difficulties endured by their children and their children's children, even as the Johnson and Dutton parents, and Guy and Eleanor's siblings, suffered mightily the deprivations, and worse, of the war that engulfed them.

I regret to say that in Paraguay I was barely aware that I had grandparents back in England or even grasped the concept of my parents having parents of their own. The realization dawned on me when my mother's much-loved father, Benjamin Dutton, died in 1945. I remember how terribly sad my mother was as she explained who her dad was, and told us about her parents, her sisters, brother, and her childhood in this somewhat mythic place called Cheshire in England. I now realized she had had a daddy and mummy, and so had my father, and that just as I had siblings, so did they, except that they were all grown-ups. It was an early glimpse that my view of the world needed expanding beyond our little Primavera.

By our later months in Paraguay, the war in Europe had ended, and we occasionally received gift packages from England, though just who these were coming from was not always clear to my siblings and me. What was clear, though, was that these rare wonders, including a little Meccano set with a clockwork motor among its components, were for sharing with our age-mates, just as everything else in this commune.

One gift was more personal, however, and initially baffling. The gift, for my birthday in 1947, was a little New Testament. The handwritten inscription read, "For dear Timothy. Much love from Grannie John in England." This gift clearly called for explanations not only of what the New Testament was, but also who Grannie John was and why she thought it important for me to have this book. Indeed, I still have it as my earliest remaining possession. Little did I realize that by the end of that year I would meet this Grannie John and other English relatives.

We passed the White Cliffs of Dover on our return to England.

Upon disembarking from our MV *Highland Brigade* at Tilbury docks on that chilly December 27, 1947, we were met by two people who were close relatives of my parents. One was my dad's mother, Daisy Johnson, whom we came to know as Grannie John and had sent me that little New Testament. She came from her home in Birmingham, England.

The other was Audrey Ann Jefferies, my mother's identical twin sister and my aunt, a relationship I only came to appreciate somewhat later. Audrey Ann had come to meet us from the Wheathill Bruderhof, which she had joined in 1943. She married Thomas Jefferies there in 1945 and the two had come to London to meet us and take us to Wheathill.

The England to which Guy and Eleanor returned at the end of 1947, familiar as it would have been in many ways, was also vastly different from the England they'd left in 1940. Though still young (midthirties on their return), they too must have been greatly changed by the physically difficult yet spiritually exhilarating venture in which they'd been such active participants. In addition, they now had a family of five young children to rear in the difficult aftermath of the punishing war, with its psychic and physical scars for all of

Eleanor with the five eldest children

England, and indeed, Europe. They would need to adapt both to the postwar social and economic challenges of the larger society and to the growing pains of the new and still evolving little community they came from Paraguay to join.

For their children, everything was strange, new, sometimes a bit intimidating, but in such matters as meeting new friends and being introduced to snow and solid ice also quite exciting.

Titterstone Clee from Bromdon by Joan Fielder

The Wheathill Bruderhof was in Shropshire in the English Midlands region on a hilly saddle at an elevation of about a thousand feet between the two main Clee Hills, Brown Clee and Titterstone Clee. The nearest real town was historic Ludlow, about seven miles west, while Bridgnorth was about eleven miles to the east. This farm country, with some wooded areas, was lovely. However, the Lower Bromdon farm, acquired for the new Bruderhof (Wheathill) after the farm's abandonment in 1942, was very rundown, albeit with some potential for both arable crops and cattle and sheep. By the time our family arrived a little more than five years later, the community had expanded in population and to its final acreage with the 1944 purchase of the adjacent Upper Bromdon farm, and in 1945, of the slightly more distant Cleeton Court farm.

Lower Bromdon in the rain

Lower Bromdon, including our second home – far end of single story building in left of photo

Altogether, Wheathill comprised 545 acres by late 1947 subdivided into numerous fields, varying in size from less than six to more than twenty acres, all separated by lovely country hedgerows. The Cleeton Court farm also adjoined the commons of the lower slopes of Titterstone Clee hill, providing access for our sheep to graze on this public moorland.

Our first home at Lower Bromdon was in two rooms of the North Wing, on the lowest level of an addition to the large main farmhouse. As in Paraguay, we had no running water in the apartment, but there was a cold-water faucet close by outside, so getting a bucket of water did not involve winching up water from a well as it had there. The community had its own little

Our first home at Wheathill, two rooms to the left of the door on the lower level addition

reservoir fed by a hundred foot borehole on an elevated field, and gravity brought the piped water down to the main buildings. As in Paraguay, we did not yet have indoor plumbing and the communal privies were some distance from the dwellings, which was mainly a problem if it was raining.

Our welcome from the good folks at Wheathill was warm, though I still recall how cold our rooms were, as were our little beds, on that first winter night of our arrival. After all, it had been high summer in the tropics we'd just left behind in South America. What heat we had in our Wheathill home was mainly from paraffin stoves, onto which we put the water bucket to take some of the chill from the water we used at our washstand.

On arrival, we children were subjected to a government-mandated two-week quarantine from other children, though curiously not from adults, in case we carried any infectious tropical diseases. We didn't, and soon we were able to meet with the other children, including a few who were slightly known to us from having been in Paraguay but having returned to England earlier. Most of our friends, however, were new.

Snow was new to us, except through such fairy tales as *Snow White*, and I found it to be colder and wetter than in my imagination! However, when our new friends introduced us to such things as sledding ("sledging" in local parlance) on some of the steep fields (the "banks") adjacent to the Lower Bromdon farmstead, we took to it happily, though we'd sometimes come home shivering and wet with frozen fingers, our flimsy wet gloves providing very little insulation.

The Crisis of 1948

While we children learnt about the bad and good aspects of winters in rural England, our parents were immersing themselves not just in the greater challenges of developing the farm and communal enterprise, but also considering, jointly with the Paraguay communities, how to be of some help addressing, in some small way, the destitution left by the recent war in Europe. The two leading brothers from Paraguay, who shared a cabin on the *Highland Brigade* with Barnabas and me, were sent over expressly to lead the assistance efforts. Hans Zumpe, a German, and Balthazar Trümpi, a Swiss national, were both sons-in-law of the deceased founder, Eberhard Arnold, and married respectively to his elder and younger daughters. Hans and Balz both held the position of servant of the word (*Diener-am-Wort*, in German) in the Bruderhof system. While this designation can be translated loosely as "minister," it often also involved substantial secular leadership responsibilities. Indeed, after Eberhard's death in 1935, Hans had been appointed as the new principal leader of the Bruderhof as it made its way from Germany and Liechtenstein to England and then Paraguay. Now, in late 1947, they were back in England to initiate and engage the Bruderhof in social and religious outreach in war-ravaged Europe.

Within little more than a month, and not long after we children had been released from quarantine and joined our age-mates at school (preschool and kindergarten), the adult membership sent Hans and Balz along with two British brothers to Germany, Austria, and Switzerland to work to relocate some displaced persons (DPs) and war orphans. One of those British representatives was Gwynn Evans, one of the two servants at Wheathill, with a background originally as a Welsh congregationalist minister. He and his wife had also spent some time in Paraguay before returning to England. The other was our father, Guy Johnson, whose legal training was a valued asset by the community in such negotiations.

Progress was being made in Europe by these four brothers, with frequent reports back to England and thence to the main community in Paraguay. I understand they generally worked as two teams, with Hans usually teamed with Gwynn and Guy with Balz, and the teams were in close contact with each other.

Meanwhile, back at the Wheathill Bruderhof, serious trouble was brewing and about to boil over. We Johnson children, along with all the other children, were largely oblivious at first to what was going on, and certainly to the underlying causes. Yet we too were scarred by the events that unfolded in the following weeks, though some much more so than others.

These problems had been developing, unknown to my parents and the other newcomers, well before our arrival. To give a brief and necessarily inadequate picture of what had been festering, the main resident servant, who had been sent with his family from Paraguay to England almost two years earlier to lead the new Wheathill commune, had developed several psychosocial problems, likely related to the stress of these responsibilities. These problems were now manifesting, though few members yet recognized what was going on. With his new responsibilities to lead this branch of the church, this servant seemed to succumb to a combination of issues, including religious zealotry and megalomania, along with great suspicion of the leaders who had just been brought in from Paraguay. It seems these leaders were also largely unaware of the undercurrents, which only broke into the open after they'd left for their mission work on the European continent in February 1948, approximately a month after our family's arrival at Wheathill.

Shortly after the team's departure for Europe, the remaining servant took actions that quickly split the commune. Though the schism lines were not entirely clear, in general his support was found more among recent members. Those he saw as opposing and challenging his actions were largely from the "old guard." This servant, when his authority was challenged on both practical and doctrinal matters, sought to place his adversaries under "church discipline" which generally meant they could not speak to other members and were separated from their families. However, the large number and proportion of adults placed in such exclusion disrupted the entire organizational structure and almost every family unit. Whether the parents were in the "in" or "out" faction mattered little since the entire church seemed to have been found "wanting."

Much of this story I only found out much later in reconstructing what had gone so terribly wrong in this "crisis of 1948." Our family situation was somewhat typical, except for the fact that my dad, who was in Europe, was initially unaware of the crisis and our plight. We children had not yet fully integrated into the new community, did not know where our mother had been sent, or what had happened to some of our siblings.

Like other families, ours was split among different locations. My father was on the "Continent." My brother and I were moved to rather spartan quarters above the horse stables at the Upper Bromdon farm. We were joined there by several other young lads in an unheated loft (except for the little heat that filtered up from the horses, along with their horsey smells!).

I hardly recall the meals at all except for breakfast, which was always a large pot of oatmeal porridge served in enamel bowls. The other meals, which we brought from the Lower Bromdon communal kitchens, seemed to include a lot of potatoes (which we'd not known in Paraguay but were a Wheathill staple), cabbage, and little, if any, meat. Our age range was from about four (my brother, Barney) to twelve for a couple of older lads. I was eight. I somehow realized that life had taken a very unaccustomed and unwelcome turn and that I needed to look out for my younger brother. In scenes resembling Dickensian novels I would later read, such as *Oliver Twist*, all of us lads tended to look out for each other as best we could. Our principal adult caretaker was a youngish and basically decent unmarried brother named Alf Withers. I think he was fairly clueless regarding how to handle and organize these young lads, but he did his best. Nonetheless, much of the time I was miserable and lonely and knew that my pals were too. Where was our mother, and where were our sisters? When would Daddy be home to rescue us?

We were instructed to keep talk among ourselves to a minimum, as it seemed that we were all being punished for some sort of collective wrongdoing. We were not, however, confined to our rooms during the day, and certainly all was not silence among us. I don't remember much of what we did, besides mucking out the adjacent cow stalls and horse stables and being assigned some work in the winter fields. We also took turns going down to Lower Bromdon to bring back food from the communal kitchen. My memory is a bit vague, and I may be conflating this with later periods, but I recall also helping with other youngsters, under the guidance of a different brother, with setting out seedlings in the nice warm greenhouse and then replanting some of these in the community garden as spring approached and the soil warmed up a bit.

We did find out bits of information on the situation from the young school-age girls, whose straits seemed even more restricted than ours. While we were at Upper Bromdon, they were housed at Lower Bromdon, about a quarter mile away through a field and a slightly wooded area we called the Wilderness, which was good for hide-and-seek and wild blackberry picking, but not in late winter!

My sister Joy recalls, "Most of us six- to ten-year-old girls slept in a large room above the granary (no longer used for storing grain). This was opposite the Main House, across a walled lawn. A young woman, Daisy, slept on a bed while we slept on palliasses [small mattresses] on the floor. During the day, each of us was sent to help with chores such as cleaning, vegetable preparation, kitchen tasks. I don't believe there were any toddler or kindergarten groups, as I guess they were in Cleeton Court with the mothers who had been moved there. I don't remember seeing either Susan or Elizabeth during that time. We were not allowed to speak except to answer grown-ups' questions or instructions. When not working, after the midday meal, we had to sit on a blanket separated from each other . . . on the 'Plateau.'" (The Plateau was a six-acre flat meadow adjacent to the main Lower Bromdon farmhouses.)

Their situation was thus apparently even worse than ours, as they basically had to sit in a circle, silently (presumably contemplating imagined sins), with very little physical or intellectual stimulation under the watchful eye of one or more of the single women. We also gathered that some of the parents, including my mother (with her two youngest children), were living down in Cleeton Court. I had only a vague notion where Cleeton Court was, didn't understand why she couldn't visit us or we visit her, never mind that I had no idea how to get there and was absolutely forbidden from asking questions!

Suddenly in April, and without immediate explanation, the cloud lifted. Families (most, at least) were together again, and our dad was back with us, trying his best to undo the damage that he knew had befallen his family as well as the community whilst he was out of the country.

How had the Wheathill crisis of 1948 come to an end almost as suddenly as it began some three months earlier? We soon knew parts of the answer, but other parts only became clearer about forty years later, and undoubtedly gaps in our collective knowledge remain.

Reportedly, my mother hiked across the moor from Cleeton Court past the village of Cleeton St. Mary to Hopton Bank, more than a two-hour hike, and mailed a letter describing the situation to Dad in Europe. I learned in 2022 that Gwynn was alerted by a phone call in Europe from Gladys Mason, wife of Arnold Mason. Dad and Balz promptly returned, were somehow able to take control of the accounts, and went to Wheathill to confront the servant, who was subsequently relieved of his duties, excluded, and, for a while, institutionalized.

Finally, some sort of normalcy resumed. We children experienced the loveliness of a Shropshire spring. Fairly quickly, Bruderhof routines resumed, including some celebrations. We were back at school and back at play, and I came to know better some of my schoolmates, including the girls, whom I had hardly known before the crisis erupted.

What was Happening in the Johnson Family?

On a wintry January 20, 1949, Mother gave birth to Jane Elfriede, (Elfriede became her preferred name later in life), at the mother house at Lower Bromdon. That day was marked also by a more disturbing event, as one of the adult men, Owen Humphreys, was thrown from one of our mountain ponies, Kitty, and suffered a compound fracture of his leg and knee. He lay in agony for some hours on

The Johnson family with newborn Elfriede

the Trefoil field, adjacent to Cleeton Court, before he was found. His leg never healed properly, and henceforth he always walked with a stiff-legged limp, and often with a cane. In my mind those events have always remained linked: first, the happy news of another little sister, and then the grim news of Owen's accident and hospitalization.[1]

Our family further expanded with the arrival, on December 29, 1950, of Christrose Carol. Another winter baby, named for the hellebore niger, the Christmas Rose, and for the season with which both this bloom and Rosie's birth were associated.

In September 1952, tragedy struck both the community and our family as a wave of polio epidemics that had been sweeping across Britain struck us. There seemed no obvious pattern for susceptibility to the dreaded disease. In our family, one of the healthiest and "bonniest" youngsters was Elizabeth, yet she was the one struck most severely. Our local National Health Service (NHS) doctor, Dr. Hodges, was initially called, then the health authorities when several children became sick with combinations of what at first seemed just to be colds, but then with severe fatigue, and then in some cases with paralysis. I still recall the visit by these health workers and the questions they asked us. Elizabeth was already showing severe paralysis, while others of us had lesser symptoms. I had heard of "infantile paralysis," but only realized how serious this situation was when these health authorities expressed their grave concerns and the need to get Elizabeth and other serious cases to the hospital. I particularly recall my mother's reaction of dread. I also remember when my sister took a turn for the worse, my parents were summoned to rush to the hospital and were told she might not survive the night. Within a few days, the most critical threat to her life had passed, but it was clear there was a long convalescence and rehabilitation ahead for her. Just how long, I did not foresee.

Back at the commune, several of us had been identified as definite or likely victims, but with lesser severity. Several youngsters were taken to hospitals. At Lower Bromdon, a hospital ward of sorts was established at our school. It became a temporary home from which most were soon released, but a

---

[1]Two years later, in 1951, Owen and his wife, Alice, became the foster parents, at Cleeton Court, to the ten German war orphans who came to the Bruderhof in the early 1950s. (See separate War Orphans addendum.) Alice was already one of our teachers, and with his physical limitations affecting what he could do on the farm, Owen eventually also became one of our teachers. I remember him warmly as the person who gave me my first chemistry book.

few stayed longer or were transferred to local hospitals. I was among the lucky ones. My case was mild and affected mainly my right shoulder area. For me, there were no serious long-term sequelae, though my shoulder remained somewhat stooped. Others were less fortunate, including our youngish school principal, Derek Wardle, who was hospitalized for some months and suffered permanent disabilities, though he was able later to fully resume his teaching and administrative duties.

After several weeks of intensive initial treatment at the Copthorne hospital in Shrewsbury, nearly a two-hour-drive from Wheathill, Elizabeth was transferred to the long-term care hospital at Oswestry, close to Shrewsbury. Altogether she was hospitalized in England for nineteen months until March 1954, with one interruption in the summer of 1953 when, though still confined to a body cast, she was allowed a brief home visit.

In February 1954, our dad was sent to the United States. His first stop was the Macedonia community in the Appalachian foothills of north Georgia to work with several representatives from the Paraguayan communities in efforts to expand the Bruderhof presence in the United States. After that stop, he traveled extensively, usually with another brother, in the run-up to a decision on a site for the first North American Bruderhof. He was heavily involved in the establishment of the Woodcrest community near Rifton, New York, and then stayed there for several months after its founding. His

c/o Maas, Gridley, California.
Dear Brothers and Sisters,   13th August, 1954

Greetings to you all this time from California!
George and I arrived in Gridley on Wednesday afternoon after a journey I would not wish to repeat but which certainly was not lacking in interest and at times excitement. I guess we shall have to reserve details for later; I've only time now for a short letter for today we must drive on to Washington as the folk at Seattle have arranged twom meetings for us for Sunday and the trip up there is estimated to take anything between 20 and 24 hours.
America is a vast continent, we drove for 95 hours t
Gridley from Woodcrest, a distance of 3139 miles through New York, Pennsylvania
Ohio, Indiana, Illinois, Iowa, Nebraska (which we almost had to re-name Waterlo
Wyoming, Utah, Nevada, into California. For those interested in statistics I
might just add that our average speed works out at 33m.p.h. for the time we wer
on the road, including small stops for gasoline and food; but if we include the
longer stops, voluntary and otherwise, we get an average of 20.9m.p.h. for the
whole trip accross took us 6 days and 6 hours. By comparison the Queen Mary
covered almost exactly the same distance in 5 days, but then of course she
didnt suffer from blow-outs!

A portion of a letter to the Wheathill community from Guy recounting his trip to California from the Woodcrest community in New York, August 1954

Macedonia Cooperative Community,
Community, Clarkesville, Georgia.

February 28th, 1954.

My Dear Timothy,
    It has been very nice to receive two letters from you;
both on the same day as the one came by ship and the other by plane!
    I was very interested in all your news, especially about
Bill Shearer. We hope he will find his way back to community from Australia
You will probably have noticed from my letter of 23rd Feb to Mummy that we
have had some quite interesting guests here too during the last fortnight.
    Macedonia is situated in a particularly beautiful part of
north Georgia, quite near the boundary of South Carolina. The school have
a photo of the whole surrounding district taken from the air. We ought to
get one of Wheathill, theyre most interesting! It seems to be practically
all mountainous woodland, with only a few patches here and there of open
pasture land. We are very high up. Even their dingles - they call them
creeks - are 1500 feet above sea level whilst the mountains vary from
3000 feet to the highest one in the whole State "Brasstown Bald" 4768 feet
This morning there was snow on these mountains, but that is the first snow
I've seen in Georgia. You see we are latitude 34 deg. N. That is about the
same as B.A. or Montevideo are, only in the other hemisphere of course.
    So the sun is hot, it is already springtime, the daffodils
have been out quite a while and buds are bursting into green. Somehow
the climate strikes me as a cross between Paraguay and England. We have
the same enormous temperature differences between midday and midnight, the
same clear starlit sky at night, as Paraguay (only different stars of course!
I have seen some beautiful birds Tim which you would have loved to see, for
instance a vivid scarlet Cardinal and a Blue bird, with bright blue back and
wings and a reddish breast. one of these hops about every morning just
outside my window. Also it can rain here as fiercely as in Paraguay, not
our gentle Wheathill drizzle which never stops from dawn till dusk but a
good old splashy downpour. But the sun soon licks it all up again!
And yet the trees and flowers are mostly those we know in England.

    Well, I'd better stop now as I've got a few more letters I ought
to write and as you can see my typing isnt particularly efficient yet!
In another fortnight Balz will be with us. Do you remember him still,
from our voyage on the old "Brigade"? We look forward very much to his
arrival as he will be a big help in the starting of the new Bruderhof,
which as I expect you know is likely to be somewhere in the North East of
the U.S.A. and not at Macedonia itself. But exactly where it will be
nobody knows yet.

    It is a great help for me Timothy on this faraway task to know
you are at home standing by Mummy in every way you can.
And now I'm already looking forward to your next letter!

    Loving greetings from your

*A letter to Tim from Guy from the Macedonia community
in Clarkesville, Georgia, February 1954*

letters were enthusiastic, and I kept a map with his accounts of his travels by car up and down the East Coast, and once out to California, and of the interesting people he was meeting.

Meanwhile, back in England, my mother was pregnant with her eighth child while simultaneously coping with family life without Dad. Fortunately, she had help from others in the community as well as from my sister Joy and me. It wasn't an easy time for her. Besides her pregnancy, she had to deal with the challenges of Elizabeth's rehabilitation, as she still required intensive assistance from her caregivers, especially my mother. I know our mother was deeply disappointed when the decision was made for my dad to remain in the United States rather than to be back in time for Rebecca's birth on October 3, 1954. He hoped he'd be back by Christmas but ended up remaining longer. But the church and its needs and decisions were, once again, paramount!

A Child's Life at Wheathill – 1948 to 1955

From their earliest years, children were conditioned to accept the values the Bruderhof emphasized. Many were not too different from the outside world, but others eventually led to conflict for some children.

Lower Bromdom, main building, south side, babies in "prams"

From infancy onward, children grew up with their age cohorts. Typically, after the baby house first year or so during which their mothers were still heavily involved in their care, they became toddlers, then kindergartners, preschoolers, and then regular school pupils.

In each age cohort, responsible adults and older teens (mostly young women) took over from parents after breakfast and shepherded their young flocks through the day for all regular activities, including both play and learning times, as well as meals, including supper, before they were returned home. This was true for both the preteen and younger children.

For many parents, the brief time between coming home from their regular day duties and having to leave again for their own communal supper was their main family time, especially during the regular work week.

Too soon, the communal bell (at 7:00 p.m., the supper bell) would summon the parents to the communal evening meals, which were often followed by meetings or

Rosie on the playground with her toddler cohort, Wheathill 1952

other communal activities. At that time, the "evening watches" would take over the care of the children. Often these watches were older girls and young women and could be thought of as roving babysitters. They would make the rounds of the homes they were assigned to and do whatever was needed to get their young charges settled, and preferably to sleep. In general, the watches were well-liked by the children, especially if they showed some tolerance for the idiosyncrasies and different needs of some members of their young flocks, including sensitivity to differences in age and temperament. Eventually, parents would come home, with at least the younger children usually already asleep, and before long it would be lights-out, even for the exhausted parents, until the morning bell would announce the start of the next day.

School

After preschool, children were advanced with considerable fanfare and with others of their age group to primary school. The number of schoolchildren varied but was never large within any given age cohort. Within classrooms there was often quite a range in age, as well as in levels of preparation. Cooperation was encouraged by teachers over competition, in line with the Bruderhof emphasis on egalitarian principles. However, there was some recognition of individual differences in aptitude and interest not only for school subjects but also in musical ability, art, athletic prowess and physical ability, and such skills as carpentry. At times, some of these areas seemed to be valued more highly than others in the prevailing communal environment, but probably less so than outside the community. Inclusion in various activities of youngsters who might otherwise be left behind was, I believe, among the more positive values imparted to children.

Cleeton Court classroom

Schooling was fairly basic, but markedly closer to nature than (as I only found out later) it would have been in a public school. Though the basic three Rs were taught in English, there was considerable emphasis from the start on some German proficiency.[2] Some of our teachers had formal teaching credentials and qualifications, others did not. Since much of our learning was, very practically, oriented toward the types of instruction most useful to an agricultural enterprise, this lack of credential may not have been a major disadvantage for most. However, I think in the early years we did lose out

School group in front of Cleeton Court

Cleeton Court outdoor class

[2]Unlike in Paraguay, where the main language among both adults and children was German, at Wheathill we primarily spoke English, though at the communal meals there was usually translation from the speaker's language to the other main language, so that most were reasonably bilingual.

on some of the instruction, especially on British history and literature, and maybe also arithmetic, that we would have been exposed to in public schools.

In partial compensation for such shortcomings, we did have constant exposure to the natural world around us, including not only our farm animals and crops, but also long walks with caring teachers who had the capacity to instill enduring interests in the flowers and birds that were a constant presence. We also enjoyed a fair quota of playtime activities, not too different from those other children would also have been having, though perhaps with a little more access to riding a couple of ponies than many children might have had.

Though life could sometimes be a bit austere, it was also true that we enjoyed at least some exposure to some of the sports that other children might engage in, including soccer, "rounders" (similar to softball in the United States), cross-country running, and several others. A particular favorite of mine, perhaps because I was more competitive in it than in most sports, was table tennis. Though not "sports" in the physical sense, three other favorite pastimes of mine were chess, stamp collecting, and simply reading for pleasure from our little school library.

Many children took up musical instruments, and some attained considerable proficiency. While my own skills, first with the recorder, and then my violin, remained rudimentary, they contributed to a deep appreciation of music which has remained with me. Our cat, Sphinx, who evidently had well-honed musical tastes, had a low opinion of my violin efforts and would quietly get up and leave our bedroom when I took up the bow. In contrast to my limited abilities, my brother, Barnabas, became a very accomplished recorder player and had an excellent ear for the piano to go along with his outstanding singing voice and whistling ability.

During our first English summer of 1948, the schoolchildren enjoyed a particular treat, traveling by lorry to the Welsh coast near Aberystwyth. A couple of large tents ("marquees") were set up — one for the boys, another for the girls — and we spent nearly a week at the seashore. We went swimming and hiking and learnt new songs and listened at night to the adventures of *Swallows and Amazons* told around the campfire.

Country dancing at Wheathill

This was a far cry from the miseries of a few months earlier! In later years, similar excursions beyond the Bruderhof's boundaries became almost an annual event. The children looked forward to these trips to the Welsh coast, or camping out near the Teme or Onny rivers in Shropshire, or, for the older children, camping and hiking in Snowdonia.

Besides these longer breaks, both adults and children would enjoy large and small group hikes on our nearby Titterstone and Brown Clee hills, or to other nearby sites, where our hiking and picnicking were often accompanied by lively group singing and country dancing.

Work

At Wheathill, shortly after my arrival at age eight, I found myself working alongside other youngsters when called upon to do so to help with various routine chores at both home and school. Parents and teachers led mainly by example, and peers expected each other to "pull one's own weight." At school, we were instructed by our teachers in maintaining our classrooms, including routine sweeping and dusting, but also such tedious and unpleasant activities (to me, at least) as periodically polishing the wooden floors with paraffin. We'd never had to do that on our dirt floors in Paraguay!

More pleasant were the daily outings into the orchards and hedgerows during the short seasons for the ripening of perishable fruits. For strawberries and raspberries, we had rows to pick from in our orchards. Blackberries we simply picked from the brambly hedges. Pleasant hours, though fewer, were also spent picking wild apples and pears as well as hazelnuts and elderberries. Some of these were for commercial sale, but most were for Bruderhof home consumption, either directly or through preparation, for instance, of jams and preserves for use in the leaner non-harvest months. At such times, the boundary between "school" and "berry picking," or even such other farm work as helping to harvest our crops of wheat, oats, barley, and potatoes, was often rather more porous than would be acceptable in non-commune life.

Farm Work

Wheathill, in the 1940s and 1950s, was a rural, principally agricultural commune, and daily life for adults and children reflected this, though as described, there were clear differences in lifestyle, language, and dress between a typical rural English village and this international and religiously based social experiment.

Ours was "mixed agriculture," with a variety of crops along with animal husbandry. Milk cows and sheep for both wool and mutton were the prime moneymakers, though we also had chickens and some pigs, along with occasional goats and ducks.

Our main crops included wheat, oats, barley, rye, potatoes, and sugar beets as well as hay for our farm animals. Our market gardening, largely for the community's own consumption though sometimes also for sale in surrounding markets, included basic vegetable crops such as lettuce, cabbage, rhubarb, kale, onions, and carrots, plus two of my least favorite: turnips and beetroot.

Our farming practices were still remarkably unmechanized and not much of a step up from the ox-wagon transport and hand tools (spades, rakes, etc.) that we'd used in Paraguay. We did have a couple of tractors (Massey-Harris and Ferguson, mainly for heavy ploughing), but the enormous Shire

Shire horses at work at Wheathill

horses were in constant use especially for carting and for harrowing, hay-raking and other duties. It would be a few more years before I would be allowed to harness and drive them for these tasks. Our equipment was not very different from most of the surrounding farms with the predominance of horsepower over tractors, though this was beginning to change both at Wheathill and more generally in rural England.

Titterstone and drying stooked sheaves of one of the grain crops

Changing seasons were a constant in nature's rhythms and defined much of our life. Crops had to be planted, with all that entailed in the preparation of the soil to

Titterstone and snowy fields

receive and sustain those annual and perennial crops through to harvest. Adults principally took on these responsibilities in communally defined divisions of labor, which also included other aspects of Bruderhof life, such as their interactions with their sister Paraguay communes, and the religious and social outreach that distinguished our commune from the rest of our rural Shropshire environment.

One of the main "crops" nurtured by the Bruderhof was, of course, their children, particularly in this very pronatalist and high fertility group. The nuclear family in which parents took primary responsibility for the raising of their own children was to some extent modified by the commune's emphasis on "community" as a social organizing principle.

As those children were maturing within the commune, they were gradually expected to take on more adult roles as they passed through the stages of childhood and adolescence.

For the boys, and outside of our little commune school, various aspects of farming mainly occupied us. Though some of this could be quite pleasant, especially if the weather was good, I personally do not have particularly warm memories of cleaning the cow stalls and horse stables, nor of planting and much later harvesting potatoes in sticky, clayey, wet mud in freezing drizzle. More interesting was the occasional assignment to take a couple of horses to an old-time blacksmith shop a few miles across the moors, beyond Cleeton Court, and watch them being shod while interacting a bit with folks off the Bruderhof. This was more fun when it involved riding the smaller and more agile ponies rather than the big, plodding Shire horses. However, driving a hay-rake pulled by one of these enormous horses as one created windrows of drying hay does bring back quite enjoyable memories of a rural life that, unknown

Guy in an older model Wheathill car

to me at the time, would soon be passing to a more mechanized future, at least in Western countries. Even at Wheathill, mechanization was developing fast.

In our first years there without electricity we relied mainly on paraffin "hurricane" and "Tilley" lights, but soon a small DC generator provided some lighting, with a larger generator installed a few years later. Though the lights were rather dim, and the generator was only on for a few hours each evening, it was progress! On the farm, horses were gradually giving way to tractors. While walking remained the main mode of inter-farm movement for children and adults alike, this was supplemented by wheeled vehicles, both for goods and people. Here too the pony trap (small carriage) that had been a frequent main transport between the Upper and Lower Bromdon farms (where most activities were headquartered), and the smaller Cleeton Court outlier, a mile away, gave way increasingly to motorized vehicles (mainly a van and small lorry).

Duty List

As we grew older, but still as young teens, our responsibilities also grew, and eventually we were included in the "duty list" or calendar of activities for the week prepared for all adults by the male work distributor and his female counterpart for duties that were not pre-assigned on a longer-term basis.

At this age, too, a more gender-based division of labor began to develop. Girls were more likely than boys to be steered toward assistance with young children and such tasks as cooking and laundry, though the lines were not always clear-cut. A seasonal task, such as the harvesting work, gave way to more gender flexibility and calls for volunteers of either sex.

Already as a preteen, but more once I reached my teen years, I'd increasingly find myself assigned to dishwashing duties after the communal meals in a room with several large sinks and other equipment adjacent to the communal kitchen. As it happens, the skills learnt there carried into later life, not only at the later communes in which I found myself in North America, but also as a part-time school cafeteria dishwasher, which I did in exchange for my school lunch (my main meal of the day) after I was later sent away from the Oaklake community in Pennsylvania in my last year of high school. But I'm getting ahead of myself.

There were a couple of other food-related duties to which I was sometimes assigned. First, in what I considered a "no win" situation, I'd take an occasional turn preparing the community breakfast, for which families would send someone, usually the father, to collect a tray of basic foods from the kitchen to take to their family for breakfast. For the preparer, some of the requirements were pretty standard, involving such things as having bread and hot water ready for pickup. Trickier was making the big vat of hot oatmeal porridge, using our coke-heated burners. Too often, mine would end up rather lumpy! I had more success with "flapjacks," which were basically oatmeal cookies prepared mostly for afternoon tea, which I was taught to make during my last months at Wheathill.

At this time, I also was assigned to assist the Bruderhof "storekeeper" on Saturdays with the coming week's distribution of food allotments to families for the meals eaten at home rather than communally in the dining hall. These foods were not for purchase, as no members had personal spending money. Rather, it was a distribution set aside for each family, based mainly on the number of mouths to be fed, but with other considerations factored in. This weekly distribution was mainly for such staples as sugar, margarine, marmite, cheese, jams and marmalade, plus sometimes some seasonal additions to go with the daily bread and porridge. A few times during the year there were pleasanter additions, such as a bottle of wine at Christmas or some other special treat that became available for distribution. One of these special treats was those flapjacks!

Another task assigned mostly to young men was to assist at the communal meals, essentially as a combination of waiters and "busboys," though I never heard the latter term until years later in the United States. People would be seated at benches at the communal tables, with basics often already set out. Communal mealtimes were very regimented. A "first bell" would have already rung about ten to fifteen minutes earlier to alert people to leave their jobs, wash their hands, and assemble for the meal, which was signaled by the "second bell." A communal song, often of religious praise in English or German, followed by a few moments of silent grace, would signal that the simple repast could begin. During the mealtime one or more assigned members would give a reading or report of some sort. Given that not all members and visitors were bilingual, an interpreter would translate what was said, so that none felt left out. Sometimes, there would instead be communal singing, often of folk songs in either German or English. Bruderhofers seemed to have an enormous variety of songs and "rounds" available, often with themes of nature and praise, but also light "nonsense" rounds. Spontaneous multipart harmony was quite common, as many of the singers were very accomplished. (Alas, unlike most of my siblings, I never quite reached that level!)

People were quite well-behaved and self-disciplined during meals, making the duties of the waiters simple. People mostly served themselves or each other from the common food containers on the table, so the waiter's main task was to replenish or replace those food and beverage containers. If the waiters, gathered at the entrance, noticed someone signaling to them, they'd quietly walk over to fix the problem, without people getting up before the meal was officially ended. The meal's conclusion was usually signaled by one or two brief public announcements and finally with another group song. At the end, we waiters would collect and sort the dishes and silverware and with other volunteers carry them back to the dishwashing area, where that crew would take over.

Lest I've left the impression that physical drudgery was the defining characteristic of my own and others' young lives at Wheathill, let me briefly note some of the more positive aspects in the Bruderhof.

True, we did not know much of the world or how it functioned. Money was something we almost never had, and the more typical school experiences of youngsters in England were something we lacked. Our limited contact with cash included some of the eye-opening experiences we did enjoy. Sometimes we would be taken to museums or ancient ruins, or to the occasional county fair. Holiday visits at scenic Welsh seaside vacation spots with our age-mates also broadened our horizons, as well as camping in the hills and vales, where we'd set up our tents, usually after first getting the permission of the nearby farmers.

We teenage boys, less constrained than the girls in interacting with outside society, also found some freedom in "off-hof" excursions by bicycle or by combinations of hiking and hitchhiking, albeit with very little pocket money. The trips never included prearranged accommodations and rarely covered even the bread-and-margarine types of food on which we subsisted. More than once, kind strangers assisted in providing basic shelter at night (such as barns), or in paying for our meals. Clearly, the world was not all evil!

We grew up basically bilingual among adults of several nationalities (albeit mostly European and white) who shared their living vision of a world free of violence within the Bruderhof and with aspirations of a better world for themselves and us. At the Bruderhof itself, the international setting led to much folk singing, and such simple but pleasant entertainment as country dancing.

Individuality within Community

While community and group activities — along with the cooperation this required — were the hallmarks of life, there was also some informal recognition of individuality and individual skills, shortcomings, and interests. For me, farm work was usually less attractive than other activities. My skills in music, woodworking, and art were at best passable. However, my general curiosity for the world around us was unbounded. Some of it was satisfied by books, and I took it as a badge of honor, even if not so intended, when other children teased me as a bookworm or know-it-all. Indeed, when we children were all given a dictionary, I was secretly pleased when the teachers gave me a less abridged dictionary than the shorter version all others got, even though I quickly had to find out what the word "etymological" in its title meant.

Children's individual interests were sometimes acknowledged through such things as Christmas or birthday gifts. While it was hard to get terribly excited by new socks, sometimes other things would arrive to cater to those more individual interests. For instance, one year I got a "how-to-do-it" chemistry and general science book, which in subsequent months gave me many hours of pleasure. True, a few of my experiments with molten lead and liquid mercury would today be banned, but those were more innocent days. Likewise, my efforts to use electricity to split water into hydrogen and oxygen, while enough to satisfy my quest for knowledge, did not start a serious fire, and only my brother and one or two friends were privy to this and some other questionable but exciting efforts to understand the hidden nature of our world.

Another wonderful gift that literally gave me a better view beyond my world was a small pair of binoculars. I had, for as long as I can remember, been fascinated by the heavens though my eyesight was rather poor. Night skies in our Shropshire hills, with no artificial light contamination, fascinated me. How lovely then to be given this device that not only magnified images but allowed me to adjust the focus! The binoculars also enhanced daytime viewing such as birdwatching, which by then had become a natural hobby for me given the variety of birds that called our woods and fields home, some year-round and some, like swallows and cuckoos, during their briefer time of summer sojourning.

An individual interest of mine, and one shared by several other youngsters, was my stamp collecting hobby. With our own early life travel and surrounded by members and transient guests from a variety of countries and cultures, I had a foundation for international interests. This was fed by collecting and sorting stamps often begged from visitors who received international mail.

As I've mentioned, philately was also the one explicit bond I had with my paternal grandfather, Edward Johnson, who was outside the Bruderhof. Through him, on the rare occasions we met, I received advice on collecting and was given a wide assortment of stamps, many dating from the previous century, along with an outdated Gibbon's worldwide stamp catalogue. I probably learned even more history and geography from that book than from my own stamp collection.

All these windows to the world beyond our communities could be seen, in retrospect, as preparing me for the possibility of a world for myself beyond the religious and geographic confines of the Bruderhof.

Overtly Religious Aspects of the Community

As I've emphasized, the origins of the Bruderhof movement were both social and religious, with the religious aspects arguably dominant from the start with what could be described as a militant Anabaptist Christian foundation to the social message of a shared life in a "community of goods." This Christian foundation was expressed in a variety of ways, including worship services that occupied a substantial portion of community attention, particularly for adults. For us children, the notion of "us" vs. "them" ("them" being the outside world) was constantly reinforced by both overt and more indirect instruction. We, the community, somehow had been shown the true and righteous path of Christian discipleship, unlike the "worldly" churches, which had strayed so far from Jesus's message (non-Christian folks were barely on our radar, as far as I remember).

The commune did celebrate, with considerable religious fervor, the two main religious holiday seasons of Christmas and Easter. While specific practices varied over time and by location, certain aspects were consistent and fairly European. Notably, Bruderhof traditions tended to have a more German than English character. Whilst for adults, the overtly religious aspects were important, for children in the Bruderhof, other aspects dominated.

Christmas

Both in Wheathill, and before that in Paraguay, the Christmas season started from the first Advent Sunday. Before dawn that morning, suitably attired angels bearing lighted candles and cookies (or other little goodies) to leave at children's bedsides would sing their way around the entire hof, visiting all children and adults. Later in the day, there would be a communal household meeting, preceded usually by a brief meeting which all but the youngest children would also attend, to hear the gospel announcement of the impending birth of the Savior. A single candle on an evergreen wreath would be lit. Outside the pattern of Sunday Advent services, we usually celebrated December 6 as "St. Nicklaus" (or Nicholas, in England) day, in which the benevolent saint and his less benevolent sidekick, Knecht Ruprecht (sometimes "Black Peter"), would bluster in with a sack of goodies to distribute, but also with a cane to threaten those the saint identified as "wanting" in the good behavior department. Like many youngsters, I was quite ambivalent about these visits. I always knew that I'd failed during the preceding year to live up to all standards yet did not consider myself particularly bad relative to my similarly situated little friends. How would I fare? I was also aware that there were rumors about this old gent and his companion, and it was true that sometimes they did bear a resemblance in demeanor and voice to more familiar local characters. Conundrums that time would resolve, but for the moment, best behavior was advised!

The next Sunday, the first Advent cycle would be repeated, starting with the angelic choir distributing those biscuits (cookies) or maybe a candy or two. The angels that entered the children's bedrooms were always female, dressed in white, though the angelic choir backing them up in four-part harmony included some masculine voices. On that second Advent Sunday, two candles would be lit at the later service. The following week, three, and then finally four candles would complete the ring of light and Christmas would be upon us!

Christmas was a special occasion, for children no less than for adults. Just before Christmas, in the anticipatory period of spiritual and physical preparation of the entire hof, each family received special Christmas rations, including the German *stollen* (a special seasonal cake with marzipan and icing), and sometimes even a little wine for the adults. The day itself would be a joyous day, with much singing to go along with the reading of relevant biblical passages. More important from the standpoint of younger children, this was the day for presents! Each child would receive one or more little gifts. Quite often, this would involve both a practical gift, such as an item of needed clothing, and another item of more personal enjoyment, such as a book or maybe even a new sled. One year I even received a real little steam-driven motor, powered by burning methylated spirits (denatured or methyl alcohol). Perhaps an introduction to physics and chemistry?

Easter

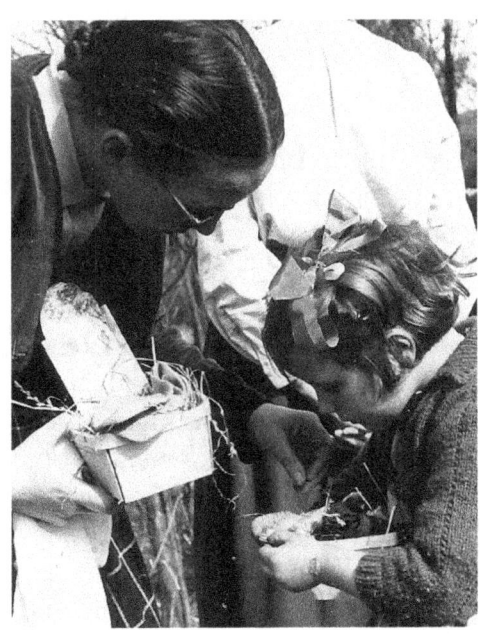

Eleanor and Rosie with Easter "nest"

Easter would arrive a few months after we'd celebrated the birth of the Christ Child. At first, whether in Paraguay or England, Easter mainly meant joyful singing and feasting along with Easter baskets for children. As I grew a little older, I sensed the less joyous aspect of the Good Friday sorrow at the crucifixion. My sense of time was underdeveloped, and at first I found it puzzling that so soon after our celebration of Christ's birth we mourned his death, and then, in just a couple of days, he was miraculously back! In time, I came to understand the logic and history a bit better.

I remember little of Easter back in Paraguay, except that sometimes there would be only one egg per person, rather than the usual two, when the chickens failed to fully cooperate in the lead-up to Easter. I do recall, however, the children's songs about the *Oster Hasen* (Easter hares) and the many beautiful religious songs of that season. There was, indeed, a sense of rebirth for the community, both in Paraguay and in England.

In Wheathill, my first Easter (1948) turned out to be my most memorable. At Wheathill, as in Primavera, there was much anticipation among children for the hunt for the Easter baskets or "nests." Typically, Easter Day began with an early morning Easter service, often including both celebratory and somber readings and songs. The service was followed by breakfast, which was a happy communal affair at Easter (unlike the usual Sunday family breakfasts which, while happy, were not communal).

That year, as in most, the children's hunt for the nests occurred a bit after breakfast. While the location of the search varied from year to year, it always involved places with ample hedges, trees, and open spaces, and sometimes other suitable hiding places. The Easter Hare was helped in his task by dads and older boys assigned to this duty, especially for nests placed in trees, which would require some climbing by the intended recipient.

On this occasion, children and adults assembled on the Plateau, which was well-supplied with trees, hedges, and bushes. Each child went looking for a nest containing, besides the eggs and other little goodies, the child's name. Some nests were placed in obvious spots, clearly intended for the youngest children. Soon the other nests were located, with word passing from one child to another about the names in unclaimed nests. Excited chattering in family groups ensued, with only one eight-year-old boy still searching for his nest and becoming quite frustrated at his unsuccessful quest. His mother and some other women sensed his frustration and soon realized that something was indeed amiss. They apparently then checked with the Easter Hare's helpers to find out who had been assigned to place this lad's nest. Oops: it seemed that no one had! The boy, while pained by the oversight, was much relieved to know this was not a punishment and somehow amends would be made.

I was that young lad! I'm happy to report that "the rest of the story" included a doubly happy ending for me. Somehow, with some scrambling by a few of the adult "sisters," a new nest was assembled and brought to me, and equilibrium restored. When I got home, I found the guilty hare had left yet another (though differently constituted) nest for me. Oh, happy day! (That nest I shared with my family.)

Other Holidays

Our other festivals, including May Day and the autumn lantern festival, were less directly religious. Indeed, dancing around the maypole on May 1 could be considered nonreligious, or at least not overtly Christian as this was also a celebration of spring and of the cycles of the year with pagan roots predating Christianity. More religious, because of the thanksgiving aspect of it, was our harvest festival, usually held in October. Some of the celebrating was done with the entire household (perhaps minus the youngest children) in attendance, and with considerable merriment, some skits, and much singing of harvest-related songs. The dining room was usually decorated with samples of our produce, including sheaves of grain, baskets of fruit and eggs, and usually an appearance by one or more farm animals, especially for the benefit of the children. There was usually also a *gemeindestunde*, or worship meeting of prayerful thankfulness for another season of produce, if not always a bounty, from the fields and orchards, and from our animals.

1955 and the Johnson Family

Dad finally returned from the United States in January 1955, eleven months after his departure, and rejoined his now-completed family. Life became temporarily more normal for us children. I was aged fifteen and dividing my time between studies for the General Certificate of Education (GCE) exams at our little community school and working in the community. At about the time I passed the only three GCEs I took, the decision was announced that our family would all emigrate to the new United States community. Therefore, rather than my expectation that I'd attend the local Ludlow Grammar School and take my "A-levels," I found myself put to work in the community office, essentially as an office boy, handling the telephone switchboard, distributing incoming mail, stamping outgoing mail, and generally assisting as called upon. Interspersed with this work, I continued what had already been part-time duty in the community's store, which handled the weekly food ration distribution to all families, and miscellaneous tasks such as clothing

The completed Johnson family with Grannie John, 1955

acquisition and distribution. My boss was the genial, though sometimes acerbic, elderly Bill Scott, but I also worked closely for a while with Arnie Tsukroff, a young American, who patiently answered my many questions about America, which I understood was to be my future home.

The community did allow me, in advance of our uncertain departure date, to continue some academic study on my own with mentoring from adults with an interest in the subjects I was intent on studying. One subject, not an official part of my curriculum, was the study of the history and geography of the United States. My main source for study was a marvelous book of political cartoons with supplemental discussions with some long-term visitors from the United States. It may not have been the most balanced of introductions, but it did give me a great sense of the diversity of political opinions throughout the history of the United States. With the help of my stamp collection, I also memorized all the presidents of the United States, in their chronological order, before ever setting foot on American soil.

Considering the Wheathill Years

Once past the rocky first few months after our arrival, our years in Wheathill were mostly good ones for me, for the growing community, and for our still-growing family. Life was a mix of school, school-related activities, and participation in the life of the community, including the main farming enterprise and the more exciting interactions with "the world." In those years, the "mission spirit" of Wheathill was strong, and our commune was the site for a number of international youth camps, which allowed us contact with these young folks. For much of this time, my father served as "guest warden" with principal responsibility for visitors, people who came from varied and often fascinating backgrounds. My dad's duties meant that very often we had these visitors as our guests at the family meals at our home, and we children took full advantage, plying them with questions and expanding our own horizons. In retrospect, despite our material poverty, this period at Wheathill was a rich time in my life.

In front of our home, summer 1955

CHAPTER 5 - 1955-1957

**Woodcrest Bruderhof, New York
to North Dakota's Forest River Colony**

The Hutterite Period

After almost eight years in Wheathill, our family was called upon to move, this time to the United States. My dad first traveled to the United States for a few months in the latter half of 1940 as part of a trip to North America to find a place for the resettlement of the Cotswold Bruderhof. While that specific objective was not achieved, he and Hans Meier did establish contacts with a couple of South Dakota colonies[1] of Hutterites and Dad managed to visit a couple of them. Those relationships were kept alive during the establishment of the Primavera hofs. The Hutterites visited Paraguay some years later and assisted in the hofs' development, bringing, among other practical goods, some bicycles for inter-hof travel.

My dad returned to the United States from February 1954 to January 1955, when he was involved in the establishment of the Woodcrest Bruderhof in New York State. Not long after his return to Wheathill, it was decided that my dad would return, with his family this time, to Woodcrest, a prospect I found exciting and looked forward to even when our departure was delayed until October.

We left England by ship out of Southampton on the SS *Italia* on October 22, 1955, my sixteenth birthday. After a brief stopover in Halifax, Nova Scotia, we sailed down the North Atlantic coast toward New York City. Ahead stood the Statue of Liberty and

---

[1]The Hutterite term, "colony," described a settlement of a small group of Hutterites established on the prairies of the United States and Canada. It is similar to the Bruderhof term, "community."

the well-recognized skyline of lower Manhattan. We arrived in our New World on the last day of October.

As we drove up the Hudson Valley to our new Woodcrest home, we noted strangely costumed children and strange candle-lit orange "masks" which we later discovered were hollowed out and carved pumpkins. This tradition of America was unknown to us, but we soon learned that we'd managed to arrive on Halloween, an American festival to which we'd not yet been alerted. Obviously, there were many mysteries yet to be fathomed!

Before leaving England, we had heard of an escalating rift in the Forest River colony of Hutterites in North Dakota between the mother colony in Manitoba and the Bruderhof-leaning members. Forest River was already something of an outlier colony of the Hutterites, the Anabaptist sect whose name the Bruderhof movement had partially adopted after first encountering them in the 1930s, but with whom there had been only limited contact in more recent years. This, though, was changing by the mid-1950s. How much the Bruderhof's establishment of a base in New York State in 1954 (Woodcrest) was a catalyst for the desire for change by some Hutterites is hard to quantify, but there was communication between the two groups by the mid-1950s. Soon thereafter there were visits and within a couple more months, in September 1955, the majority of Forest River members elected to join the Bruderhof, including John Maendel, one of their two ministers. The minority, in accordance with an edict from the council of ministers, returned to Manitoba as faithful members of the Hutterian church.

That crisis initially seemed unrelated to the Johnson family. However, our delayed departure from England to Woodcrest contributed to a change of plan destined to affect our family. We learned, shortly after our arrival at Woodcrest, that our dad, a new and still "unconfirmed" servant of the word, was to assist in guiding the new Bruderhof venture at Forest River and our family would travel there soon.

Despite this impending move, preliminary arrangements had been made for the older children to enroll in the local public school system. Though I did visit Kingston High School, I did not formally attend. Beginning school only to leave within two weeks didn't seem to make sense. Instead,

I joined Dad as he drove down to Philadelphia to meet Ed Potts and family and spend a couple of days in the area.

At that time, immigrants had to have a sponsor in the United States. Ed Potts, a Quaker living in Philadelphia and brother of Tom Potts, a recent Bruderhof joiner, had agreed to serve as our sponsor. Our meeting with his family, and seeing his American home, confirmed the positive aspects of the people and potential educational opportunities from my dad's United States travel reports and excited me about our move.

Thus, two weeks after our arrival at Woodcrest, the Johnson family set off for North Dakota from New York by overnight train via Pittsburgh to Chicago with a total contingent of about twenty people. After a layover visit to the Chicago Botanic Garden (lots of chrysanthemums in November!), we took another train to Minneapolis-St. Paul where we switched to a rather nice Greyhound Scenicruiser bus to Grand Forks, North Dakota.

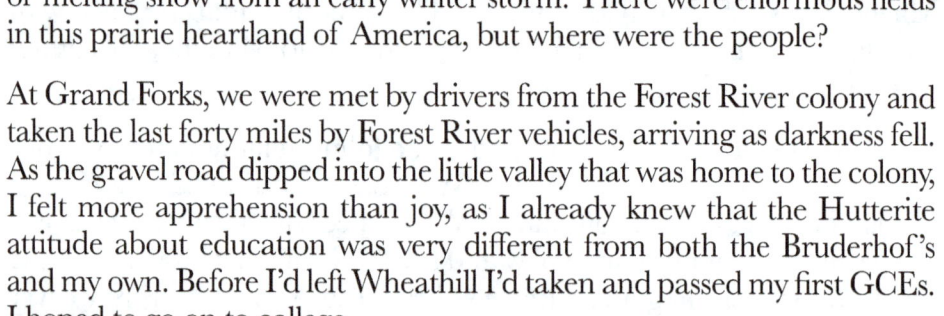

The trip was long and tiring, but also interesting. I was a bit dismayed to see how flat the terrain became, and how in Minnesota there were patches of melting snow from an early winter storm. There were enormous fields in this prairie heartland of America, but where were the people?

At Grand Forks, we were met by drivers from the Forest River colony and taken the last forty miles by Forest River vehicles, arriving as darkness fell. As the gravel road dipped into the little valley that was home to the colony, I felt more apprehension than joy, as I already knew that the Hutterite attitude about education was very different from both the Bruderhof's and my own. Before I'd left Wheathill I'd taken and passed my first GCEs. I hoped to go on to college.

Yet, as we stepped out to meet the bearded men in their severe dark clothing and the women with their long dresses and *kopftuch* headgear, I knew I'd have to put off any such personal aspirations for at least a few years. I felt stranded in a cold, flat, and strange world, where my future would probably be in farming and manual labor more than in teaching or other more intellectually stimulating pursuits that I had dreamt of at Wheathill. Had I dropped out of school in England to spend my teen years, and perhaps beyond, in this forbidding setting? The choice had not been mine to make, and now I had to make the best of it. I think that was also the unspoken sentiment of my siblings, and perhaps even my parents.

And yet, we could hardly have asked for a warmer welcome than the one we received that evening, and in subsequent weeks, as we came to know our new hosts.

Forest River, North Dakota

The next weeks were a jumble of mixed and sometimes contradictory impressions of the Hutterites and their lifestyles and of their efforts to adapt to the more modern Bruderhof ways they had recently decided to adopt, even as we also struggled with our own challenges of adapting to this setting, so different from rural England in so many ways!

All of us now at Forest River — Hutterite and Bruderhof, those from the United States and those from England — were on uncertain ground in this new situation. However, the significant impact of the weather and the real demands of a large farm with a short growing season during which it had to feed the colony for the remainder of the year overrode many of the cultural expectations of a traditional Bruderhof community, including those around education and engagement with the outside world.

That said, many of the outer forms of the daily routines in North Dakota were similar to our Wheathill lives. One example was the distribution of duties, albeit now tailored to a much larger and more mechanized farm operation. Mealtimes, in terms of communal dining for most lunches and dinners, and in meal preparation and then cleanup, were also similar to Wheathill, as were the children's "departments," but these diverged more as children entered their teens, with both earlier Hutterite culture and practices and the realities of operating a large agricultural operation contributing to these divergences.

Arriving at the start of a North Dakota winter presented its own set of new challenges. I remember within a couple of days of our arrival having to figure out, with my dad, how to put up storm windows, and then also fix clear plastic sheeting for additional insulation against the penetrating cold. Our house had only one stove and it burned wood and lignite, a fairly plentiful, but low-quality coal mined in parts of North Dakota. Our only warm water was from a bucket placed on the

Our Forest River house

stovetop. "Plumbing" was an outhouse, perhaps sixty feet from our front door, though later we improvised with a bucket toilet under the stairs for those unable or reluctant to brave the freezing outhouse!

With the help of our new Hutterite neighbors (all very helpful, even when bemused by our "English" ignorance on matters that were second nature to them), we figured out how to clean the chimney's interlocking sets of

Hans Meier

sooty metallic pipes that snaked upward through the house to release the heat from the stove in our living room.

Also in those first few days, we experienced some of the dissonance that was often to bubble to the surface as these cultures met and sometimes clashed. Take the matter of musical instruments as an example. In the Bruderhof, musical instruments and what could be considered folk singing, in German and English, were integral parts of the community's daily life. However, when Hans Meier (the visiting senior Bruderhof servant when we arrived) played a Mozart duet on his violin with my brother, Barnabas, on his recorder during the "love meal" (a special meal) held for our newly arrived group, it caused a considerable stir. A lengthy discussion ensued on why the Hutterites rejected such music, and indeed most nonreligious singing, whilst the Bruderhof enjoyed both instrumental music and multipart harmonious singing, not limited to religious services or songs. While the emerging consensus clearly favored the Bruderhof position, there were residual undercurrents of ambivalence and dissent.

Only a week or so after our arrival I had yet another unexpected new experience. I was awakened late one night to join my dad and most of the colony's men to catch and load onto an enormous, enclosed truck (leased for this event) nearly the entire flock of over six hundred turkeys, by the dim barn light of one or two bulbs, plus a kerosene light or two outside. Thanksgiving loomed, and the beautiful big birds were destined for American tables in a holiday ceremony I had not yet fully grasped. I was told the reason the truck arrived only late in the evening was both because the well-fed toms would be relatively easy to handle in their somewhat sleepy state and because the colony would be paid by the fully loaded weight of the truck, minus its initial weight, and the tom turkeys had just had their evening meal, but had not yet digested it fully, so in a sense we were getting credit for the weight of what by morning would become their excrement. Clever chaps, those farmers!

The turkeys were not only large, but also understandably had strong objections to leaving their warm barn quarters to be hoisted by their back legs through bitter cold subzero night air into the truck. Perhaps, their walnut-sized brains notwithstanding, they had some premonitions of their imminent fates. Certainly, they put up strenuous resistance, and people like my dad and me, with no prior experience controlling a wing-flapping thirty-pound tom, found it quite a challenge. My dad was smoking his hand-warming briar pipe during this exercise, until the flapping wing of one of the objecting birds managed to knock his pipe out of his mouth and halfway across the barn, to the amusement of Josh Maendel and others, and to my dad's chagrin!

When the task was completed and the turkey-laden truck had left, the tired but exercise-heated men made their way to the communal kitchen for a well-deserved high-calorie meal (bread, butter, various meat cuts), washed down by some of their colony-produced homemade beer and wine. By the time my dad and I finally took the short walk home close to 3:00 a.m., the temperature had dropped to about twenty below (Fahrenheit), and the night stars danced above us!

From the start, I found myself much engaged with the youth of the colony. With Hans-Uli Boller, who was several years older and had a more formal leadership role as an already-baptized and well-respected member of the Bruderhof, I found I had a major role in setting up the youth group somewhat in the pattern of the one I'd left in Wheathill. Most of the young men and women seemed excited to be learning from each other and sharing new experiences. Unsurprisingly, not all was harmonious and sometimes there were differences to be ironed out, particularly in dealing with more traditional group members who were obviously uncomfortable with the social mingling of the sexes, and with such group activities as ice hockey, group hikes in the snowy valley, bonfire sing-alongs on the frozen river ("tools of the devil!"), and some folk dancing along with the occasional musical instrument. Generally, we coped, even when some may have been less comfortable than others.

The bitter cold of our first North Dakota winter seemed to seep into almost everything we did. The lines from Christina Rosetti's poem, *In the Bleak Midwinter,* "snow had fallen, snow on snow," could often have been our adage. A notable and memorable example, for me and other ill-clad shepherds and angels, was the first Christmas Eve pageant, held in the cowbarn, where we were protected from the wind, but the air was cold enough that the water troughs were caked in ice. The ceremony was lovely, with candlelight bathing the holy couple, the baby, the animals, and us assorted angels and shepherds, but by the time the Christmas story had been read, I was not the only one close to passing out from hypothermia. I'm sure the original Bethlehem was not this cold!

More significant for me, though, than such matters as cold weather was the problem of continuing formal education. The Hutterites traditionally did not continue formal schooling beyond about age fifteen in their "German" (Hutterisch dialect, somewhat akin to Yiddish) schools. Some of us young folks, and some of our elders, both among newly arrived Bruderhof parents and some Hutterite parents, were eager for their children to progress beyond eighth grade.

An initial compromise was to allow us to take high school correspondence courses through the North Dakota State Agricultural Extension Service while also working at the commune. Soon, this approach was recognized as being inadequate, and those above elementary school were permitted to attend the local public high school in the tiny town of Inkster, five miles by road from the commune, from early 1956. The whole high school had only forty students, even with the infusion of the eight colony kids! I was glad to attend the public school and enjoyed interacting with American students and the American curriculum and I got on well with the three high school teachers.

Life on the big North Dakota colony revolved not just around the church, but necessarily around the constant hard work required to make a living. While this could be very difficult, and certainly different from the way we'd farmed in England, it was also exciting in its own way. We were surprised at the level of responsibility vested in quite young children in such matters as operating the farm machinery. In England, I could not be a licensed driver until age eighteen, yet here, within a week, my young Hutterite friends started me driving tractors and farm trucks and my twelve-year-old brother and I happily learned to maneuver the little John Deere M tractors through their paces as we transported goods to different farm departments. In North Dakota, driving permits could be obtained at age fourteen, but most Hutterite males were already quite accomplished tractor drivers by about the time they reached ten. Josh Maendel, at seventeen the most senior lad in my immediate circle, was probably the most accomplished driver of the big caterpillar-track type TD-18A tractor and his skill was highly respected by more senior men. I was amazed how gently he could maneuver the big hydraulic blade to raise snow around the houses to windowsill level to provide additional insulation against the bitter blizzards, and I felt honored to be with him on that tractor, learning how one manipulated the levers to accomplish the complex tasks involved in such an enterprise.

A few weeks after our arrival, my brother and I took the smaller John Deere model M tractor across the river to cut and bring in firewood. The tractor engine overheated, so we turned off the motor, and added river water to the cooling system. When we restarted the motor, the tractor sputtered to a halt and would not restart. We'd unwittingly added the water to the fuel tank! Our new Hutterite friends were unimpressed by these English lads but quickly helped us move up the steep learning and survival curve of operating these types of machinery. Later, I became fully integrated into the plowing, harrowing, and harvesting routines, along with caring for the cattle, pigs, and particularly chickens, which necessarily occupied so much time and effort on the main and satellite colony farm — the "East Farm" near the Red River and leased by the Forest River colony. It was unoccupied all winter but very busy with planting, growing, and harvesting the rest of the year. (No livestock were kept at East Farm, though.) Total arable land for the combined main colony and East Farm was 7,000-plus acres, which greatly exceeded the 545 total acres at Wheathill.

In those first few months after Forest River's formal expulsion by the Hutterites in late 1955, the commune experienced rapid changes as it transformed into a Bruderhof. Among the more obvious changes was a rapid influx of Bruderhofers, first from Woodcrest (along with our family from Wheathill) and then increasingly from Paraguay. In early 1956, this included what were often referred to as the "Primavera boys," a half dozen young single men brought in to help with the farm operations. They, in part, replaced some Forest River men who had either returned to their Manitoba Hutterite mother colony or joined the Bruderhof but had

Michael Caine, one of "the Primavera boys," with Tim

been relocated to Woodcrest. These moves had both intended and less predictable consequences, both for their individual participants and for the local commune cultures.

Another obvious change was in the use of transport, especially as new non-Hutterites arrived bringing their cars. Farm mechanization had already been adopted by Hutterites, so tractors and trucks were widely used, as also were labor-saving equipment such as milking machines. In almost all cases, these were operated by men only. In particular, women were still not permitted to drive. With the arrival of newcomers, who generally brought with them their non-Hutterite and less traditional social and economic values, rules like this began to shift. Before long, several cars and passenger-friendly panel trucks were communally available to both men and, gradually, to women. These included the little Studebaker which I (only recently myself licensed to drive!) taught my sister Joy to drive, and a secondhand Cadillac hearse that was brought by a young couple from an Indiana Brethren congregation. While this black hearse looked a bit incongruous among the other Forest River vehicles, it turned out to be quite practical. Actually, even before their arrival with their young family with the intention of joining Forest River, Arden and Vivian Morris had begun to modify the hearse into a more family-friendly transport. And, some months later, I became unexpectedly well-acquainted with this vehicle in its modified form.

Life in North Dakota was dominated by the weather, a new reality, especially for those used to England. Winters came early and were, at times, bitterly cold. Loading alfalfa bales from the previous summer onto trucks and then feeding these to the cattle was never fun, but even less so in sub-zero blizzard conditions! A couple of times I was involved also with other young colony men in driving to the Dahlen rail stop, a few miles west of the colony, where we shoveled lignite from the railroad freight cars onto our trucks to replenish the colony's supplies of this rather smoky heating fuel. I remember that despite the subzero cold we found ourselves sweating with the physical exertion, and that even in those frigid temperatures, beer could be quite refreshing!

By midwinter, when the layers of ice on the river were thick, so was the depth to which the soil froze solid. It was obviously important to bury water pipes deep enough to keep them from also freezing solid. For me, the extreme depth of winter's frozen ground was brought home when Forest River experienced a midwinter death in February 1957. Rachel Maendel (usually addressed as Rachel "Basel," a respectful title for senior women) was a widow and the mother and grandmother to several at Forest River, including some I'd come to know very well. A backhoe had to be used to break through the thick layer of icy soil, as spades and shovels were no match for these conditions, before the simple coffin could be lowered into the grave at the little burial site.

But winter did end and that brought with it new challenges. For example, spring's warmer temperatures meant mud! The subsoil remained frozen solid well after the surface layer thawed, so the melting snow had at first nowhere to drain away to on these flat plains. It was true for both our graveled roads and for our fields, and in both cases seriously interfered with vehicular movement. Tractors had limited traction once their big wheels cut through the muddy surface to the underlying ice layer. They would spin ineffectually if hauling a heavy load or if plowing through heavy soil. Over time, the Hutterites and other local famers had developed practical solutions, or workarounds, some of which I absorbed, inadvertently learning lessons of applied physics and other disciplines. Time, and longer days, also soon helped carry us through these seasonal difficulties.

Another more delayed effect from the thawing snow was the localized flooding caused as the usual modest flow of our Forest River coped with the much-increased meltwater flow from upriver. This flooding was a more serious problem in our second spring than in our first, with a combination of the breakup of the heavy ice that had built up on the river and the large flow of water that was carrying the ice blocks downstream, sometimes creating ice dams behind which the water would rapidly rise. In this case, as the swirling waters pooled behind our cattle barn, some of the men had to take rapid action both to rescue some semi-stranded cattle and also to do what they could to protect some smaller structures that were now in the path of the unexpectedly high water.

Difficult and different as Forest River could be, it also had some compensating aspects. For me, those definitely included the often clear, brilliantly starlit nights and the frequent appearances of the aurora borealis, the wonderful northern lights. These could appear at any time of year, not just in the long nights of the northern winters. Indeed, I recall more than once when working the fields during the spring and summer, turning off the lights of the big John Deere diesel tractor and dismounting the tractor to let my eyes grow accustomed to the darkness, the better to survey the major constellations, the magnificent Milky Way, and those awe-inspiring northern lights, which I'd never seen in England. And, as a special treat for quite a while, our nights had an unexpected visitor, my first good comet. During that period, along with other popular western -type American folksongs, we also learnt the American folksong "Home on the Range." We were now on the great prairie, and the occasional "deer and antelope" would be found foraging around our Forest River valley. The verse from that song that most resonated for me was, "How often at night, when the heavens are bright with the light of those glittering stars / Have I stood there amazed . . . ," its expression of wonderment at the mystery of the heavens echoing my own. The heavens were ours to enjoy and ponder, and I did, even if other lines in the song — "where seldom is heard, a discouraging word . . . ," — did not always seem to apply in our own "home on the range."

Elizabeth with the community bell, rung to call the community to meals and other gatherings, summer 1956

The question of balance between colony life and the surrounding world was often an issue, and perhaps particularly so for those who had a non-Hutterite background because they were now at the interface between "the world" and "the colony." This question of balance was true for most of the students now allowed to attend the public school in Inkster. Most of the time, and for most of these students, the colony's needs took precedence over other considerations.

Elizabeth, Reve Le Blanc and Moses Baer, Spring 1957

In particular, all recognized that farms require constant work, albeit with different seasonal patterns for major crops and for raising cattle, pigs, and chickens. It was the expected pattern, developed by Hutterites (and farm communities more generally) over generations, and we newcomers also generally adapted to these patterns. Thus, I took my cues from my young male age-mates and older brothers as I learnt the ropes of the various farm departments, as well as with other duties assigned by the work distributor. Much of the work was new to me, and both challenging and interesting as new experiences with a different type of agriculture from my English background. For one thing, the scale of operations was completely beyond anything I'd experienced, as I soon found myself driving big diesel tractors on long fields, tilling in one half-day shift a far greater acreage than our smaller English tractors could even manage in a day in the heavier clayey soil of Shropshire!

Though we'd be required to plow, harrow, and plant the fields (or undertake other farm duties) for a few hours when we came home on most school days, longer shifts were sometimes required either when we were temporarily assigned to stay home from school, or even more when the Inkster school let out for the summer so that all the local farm kids would be available for much of the short northern growing season. At Forest River, this was also when some of us were assigned temporarily to the East Farm satellite farm, almost twenty miles away, to provide the intensive effort required to prepare the soil for planting.

"Work, for the night is coming when man's work is done," a line from a song often sung at Wheathill, would have seemed particularly appropriate here except that for a few weeks work would continue right through the night, illuminated by our tractor lights. The only "recreation" I recall was a couple of brief dips in a small pond that served as a swimming hole at East Farm. However, I do recall an odd experience while out on the tractor one night, a mile or two from the base farm building we slept and ate in and to which I needed to return when my shift ended at midnight. It was daylight when I started my twelve-hour shift and could see the farm. Now, well after nightfall, my daytime landmarks had disappeared, and I suddenly realized that I could not pick out the dim lights of the farmstead from other dim lights on the horizon. Overhead was the canopy of stars from which at least I could determine where north was and the general direction I'd need to go. Indeed, I did get back, but in the process learnt some lessons about advance observation, planning, and navigation!

Some weeks later, and back at the main colony, another midnight start to another long shift ended prematurely for me with a tractor accident at 5:00 a.m. on July 26, 1956, requiring an emergency trip to the little Grafton Hospital in an adjacent county. I was stitched up and a plaster cast applied. No more tractoring for me until that cast could be removed a few weeks later.

What I could assist with, after a couple of days of immobility, was the quite large-scale (at least compared to that at Wheathill) chicken-raising enterprise. Besides the small numbers of poultry needed for the colony's own consumption, they had a much larger commercial business for both eggs and meat. Increasingly, I found myself helping Pete Hofer, the "chicken boss," first with less physically demanding aspects of the complex tasks of raising several thousand chickens, such as cleaning and sorting the eggs collected daily from the different levels of the multilevel chicken barn. Soon, more physical duties, such as feeding the poultry, were added, especially once the cast was removed. Though I never aspired to becoming a chicken farmer, chickens henceforth became a major subtheme of my remaining time in North Dakota.

In discussing Forest River, and contrasting it with Wheathill and Woodcrest, I have dwelt on its isolation from the wider world but also its wish to move closer to that world while not abandoning wholesale its own traditions and legacy within the Anabaptist movement. Along with its moves to a merger with the Bruderhof, Forest River also increasingly reached out in other ways. In the first months after our arrival, all residents found themselves to be "participant observers" to some of this outreach, and increased contact with the outside world, and its obverse of that world's interest in this group.

First, and within the earliest months after our arrival, we began to have occasional visits by some faculty members and their students from the University of North Dakota in Grand Forks, about forty miles from the colony. I do recall interesting discussions with a few of these students and their mentors, and hope both sides did gain something from the interchanges!

The second example was a few months later, in the summer of 1956. It involved the participation of four Forest River high schoolers in a Quaker-sponsored (AFSC) youth camp at a retreat in central Iowa, focusing particularly on issues of world peace and justice. I'm unsure how Forest River came to be invited and was surprised at my own inclusion though delighted by the opportunity to engage socially and educationally with other Midwestern youngsters as well as United States and foreign lecturers, several of whom were affiliated with Quaker colleges. We bunked in sex-segregated cabins also shared by our faculty/mentors. In addition to the formal presentations and discussions, we managed smaller group discussions on various topics. One of my cabinmates was a young Black lad from adjacent Missouri who helped open my eyes to some of what it was like to be a young Black in the 1950s in a still heavily segregated area (thanks, Ladell Crawford!), something I'd barely been exposed to in North Dakota.

Two from our Forest River group were from the traditional Hutterite background, Josh Maendel and Katy Maendel, and I know it was a particularly eye-opening experience for them. So also, I suspect, was the casual and certainly very non-Hutterite garb of most participants, along with the coed swimming in a big open-air pool. The garb and coed situations were not new to me, nor to the other young non-Hutterite Bruderhofer, Virginia Ostrom. But for all of us, this was a wonderful experience, and we were sorry to have to part from our new friends as the conference ended and we bade them farewell.

At that point, by prearrangement, we were met by two novice Bruderhofers, Marion and Howard Johnson, previously affiliated with the Koinonia cooperative/commune in southwest Georgia, for the long drive back with them to North Dakota via a somewhat circuitous route, providing us with a few additional new experiences.

The trip took us first to an overnight stop with a Quaker family in Ames, Iowa, and then on to eastern Iowa, near Cedar Rapids. There we visited a couple of the religion-based Amana communities which, by then, were already known for some of their cooperative manufacturing activities, including Amana refrigerators and other electronic devices, as they evolved beyond their original but quite progressive farming roots into new lines of cooperative industry. Were there lessons here for Forest River and similar groups? Time would tell, and indeed when some decades later I was back in that area, I was able to visit again and saw that the enterprise seemed to be continuing to adapt and evolve quite nicely in their villages.

We headed next, at nightfall, into Minnesota. Dead tired and with deepening darkness, we simply pulled out our sleeping bags at the side of the road to settle in for the night. At some point, Josh and I awakened to some sort of ruckus. Some curious cattle had wandered into our encampment and disturbed the women, as did the sight of ghostly forms we had not seen earlier but which were now visible by the light of the late rising, almost full moon. After successfully shooing away the cattle and belatedly realizing that they were separated from the road and us by a fence, we then checked on our silent observers, who were gathered not far from us and seemed in no way threatening. Indeed, they weren't! It turns out we'd actually bedded down in the dark at the edge of a roadside cemetery and the dim light of the moon now revealed our ghostly neighbors as grave markers. Fortunately, none of us were particularly superstitious. Before long we were on the road again.

Still in Minnesota, we paid a brief visit to Rochester's famed Mayo Clinic (until then unknown to me) before continuing to Minneapolis. Heading farther north, via Sandstone and in a rural area in the general direction of Duluth, we stopped at the home of a man known well to Howard from earlier years, perhaps his military service days. Carroll King had since become a Minnesota state legislator. He was a very thoughtful man from whom I learnt a bit about state-level government. He would eventually step away from politics and join the Bruderhof.

The final leg of our return across northern Minnesota included quick stops at Lake Itasca to visit the source of the mighty Mississippi River, which here was just a little river, and at Bemidji, where a stop at a colorful statue of Paul Bunyan and Babe, his blue ox, introduced us to some of the folk tales and mythology of the region. Then back into North Dakota and our late evening return to our community home, but not without some warm memories and, perhaps, some intimation of future possibilities beyond Forest River.

This eleven-day experience was surely the highlight of my entire North Dakota period. In part, it was simply because it was a break from the routines and stresses of colony life. It also served my interest in knowing better at least some aspects of America, with better insights into its history, its politics, its geography and, most of all, its wonderful variety of people.

The day after our return, at the communal midday meal, the four of us were welcomed back and asked to give a report on our travels. We started a bit hesitantly, but our report was enthusiastically received, and soon we warmed to the task as we fielded questions about the youth retreat and our other travels, each from our different perspectives. Some of our responses elicited laughter, which in general I found in short supply at Forest River. Instead of reporting at only one communal meal, we ended up doing a couple of additional days and, despite our hesitant start, found ourselves enjoying the interactions with our appreciative audience.

Most folks at the commune favored increased outreach into the world around us, and I think the positive feedback to our report was an affirmation of their decision to encourage the trip. I'm not sure, though, that some of the more traditional members were equally enthusiastic about some of our observations, which related to a broader range of issues the Bruderhof was grappling with, some of which would vex the Bruderhof/Hutterite relationship in the months to come.

I returned to start my senior year in the fall of 1956, eager to attend to my academic studies. However, each day we had to go to work at the colony right after our

Tim's Senior portrait, taken just before Forest River removed him from high school

return from school, and when the farm work needed us, we would be withheld from school altogether. I was not the only one who questioned this mandate, but I was seen as the lead in pushing for more attention to our academic work. I was also seen by some at the commune as "not being in the right spirit," religiously. While to that "sin," I had to plead guilty, it took me by surprise when the Bruderhof leadership's response was to force me to drop out of school at the start of 1957 with less than a term to complete before graduation. For me, this was a bitter pill and was done over the additional objections of the high school's principal, Mr. Day, who considered me a star student.

Thus, I went to work full-time, and given my tractor injury experience, I became the "chicken boss," responsible for the commune's four thousand or so chickens and preparing them and their eggs for market. Not at all what I'd planned.

Though my withdrawal from the public school was a very painful blow to me and distressing even to my Inkster teachers, in retrospect it was probably a well-disguised blessing, albeit not the one so intended by those who decided on this drastic action.

A major source of tension was related less to the Hutterite/Bruderhof intrinsic cultural differences than to the necessity of recognizing North Dakota's very short agricultural growing season and the enormous effort required during that season — preparing the soil, planting crops in quick but orderly succession, harvesting the produce — on several thousand acres of the main farm and the East Farm. The Hutterites knew this, and knew that the men would often have to work day and night in the fields and barns and could not stop for spiritual clarifications, worship meetings, and so forth. Some Bruderhofers, perhaps feeling spiritually superior in doing so, felt that the essential "spirit" was somehow being made subservient to the need to "make hay while the sun shines." The more practical Hutterites, like all neighboring farmers, knew that there is a time and place for the different components of life, and could be quite frustrated by the apparent Bruderhof blindness to such facts of rural Midwestern life. A consequence of all these tensions was that the financial situation of the deeply mortgaged colony was deteriorating rapidly, due to inadequate attention to the farming reality of those at Forest River who espoused the standard Bruderhof line that "God will find a way," a perspective not shared by some members or by the external creditors.

By the spring of 1957, the dissolution of the Forest River experiment was only a matter of time, and the search for a new Bruderhof site went into high gear. Soon a suitable site was identified in southwest Pennsylvania. Most of the Forest River members decided to make this move, with a smaller group determined to try to salvage and reorganize Forest River. Our family was among those planning to leave.

Our last few weeks were painful and remained so in the memory of those caught up in the ugliness for many years after the split. The colony went into some sort of receivership, the details of which have faded from my memory, but I do recall some of the bewildering events, such as an auction to which neighbors and even some South Dakota colonists came. My brief diary notes for March 22, 1957, refer to the auction as an "absolute flop," in which not much more than a thousand dollars of equipment and other holdings were auctioned off. By some sort of prior arrangement, the auction was halted and the equipment and acreage that was up for sale were retained since the offers did not reach some preset price levels.

Meanwhile, on the hof, there were strange goings on, with separate meetings of the two main factions — those who were about to leave versus some of the established old guard who understandably wanted to retain and salvage as much as they could in this debacle. People, who until recently had been "brothers and sisters," were hardly talking to each other, though some on both sides did try to mitigate some of the disaster that such a split in the middle of the growing season seemed to entail.

Building tensions within the Forest River commune culminated in the June 1957 departure of fifty to sixty of us, the Bruderhof segment and more than half of the commune's inhabitants. I recall that strange day, June 21, when I left. Almost all the Bruderhof faction had already departed for a temporary New York State location. I left that day in the final departure group as one of three drivers of our black Cadillac hearse, brought to Forest River by Arden and Vivian Morris and repurposed as an ambulance to transport my cast-bound sister Elizabeth, along with my mother as her main caretaker. To me, Forest River looked empty and forlorn as we drove out of that valley, the last vehicle to head eastward to rejoin the main group. Our departure was about nineteen months after our arrival on that chilly November evening. I could not help but reflect on the contrast with the optimistic enthusiasm with which we'd been welcomed.

The calendar showed we were at the summer solstice. Summer had just begun, as had a new chapter in my own and my family's lives.

CHAPTER 6 - 1957-1958

North Dakota to Pennsylvania: "Consequential" Moves

Things Fall Apart

The last of the Bruderhof faction of the colony departed North Dakota early on Friday, June 21, 1957. There were eight of us, including Arden Morris, who had brought our vehicle, a converted but still solid-black 1948 Cadillac hearse to Forest River when he and his wife, Vivian, arrived some months earlier. Arden, Peter Hofer, and I sat in front, as the three drivers and navigators.

Our group was separate from the main, earlier-departing groups in part because my ten-year-old sister, Elizabeth, had recently undergone, in Minneapolis, the second of two spinal fusion operations to correct scoliosis from the severe polio she'd suffered nearly five years earlier in England. She was immobilized in a light body cast, which made travel by buses, trains, and ordinary cars impossible. The combination station wagon/ambulance into which the hearse had been converted, still with side curtains for privacy and a platform bed, could accommodate Elizabeth. My job, besides sharing in driving and navigation, was to physically carry Elizabeth to and from this vehicle whenever we made stops requiring such moves. Her main caregiver, of course, was my mother, Eleanor, who mostly stayed in the back of the hearse with Elizabeth, along with three younger girls, including two of Arden Morris's daughters, and my youngest sister, Rebecca (then known as Becky), who was not quite three years old.

Though June 21 dawned fairly clear, during the previous night there had been severe storms and we heard on the radio of tornado casualties in

Fargo, where we were to cross the Red River from North Dakota into Minnesota. As we entered Fargo, I saw for the first time the amazing destructive force of a tornado. This one had leveled a considerable swath of the buildings along our road, and I believe nine people had perished. Many people suffered injuries and there was massive property damage. We were waved on by the rescue crews, so did not linger, but the images of destruction certainly did.

We turned east and crossed the Red River of the North into Moorhead, Minnesota, and headed to Minneapolis. We spent that night bedded down in the home of the Crocker family, who earlier had hosted my mother during my sister Elizabeth's spinal fusion surgeries in Minneapolis and then had visited Forest River for a few days two weeks prior to this stay. It must have been quite an imposition on them, with four adults and four young girls, but they handled it very graciously.

Early the following morning, June 22, we set off on the next stage of our journey and were soon well into Wisconsin. Unfortunately, near the little town of Tomah, near Wisconsin Dells, the metal rim of one of our wheels blew out, as did the tire. We could not continue until we were able to scour a local car graveyard for a wheel of the unusually large diameter of our Cadillac hearse. After several hours, we found a replacement (on a junked pre-WWII Lincoln, if

memory serves), and replaced the damaged wheel and tire. It was approaching nightfall by the time we got back on the road, exhausted by our tedious hours of unexpected frustrations. Arden Morris, Pete Hofer, and I took turns driving and napping, while Mother and the four children mostly slept in the back. I recall how dead tired I was as I drove through Aurora, Illinois, toward Chicago. It was at about that point that we drivers all sensed that something was very wrong with the engine, which was gradually losing power. I don't know what time it was, but possibly 3:00 or 4:00 a.m. with no garages open along the way. We decided that we'd better stop and nap for a couple of hours until daylight to get a better sense of the problem and our next steps. It was a strange sort of fitful sleep, at least for me, waking intermittently behind the wheel, with a helpless feeling that I was unable to steer, before realizing I didn't need to, and lapsing back into a doze. It was now Sunday morning, June 23.

We still had a little power propelling us forward when we resumed our journey after daylight. We decided to try to make it on Route 30 past the little town of Plymouth, Indiana. It was, of course, in the days before interstate highways, and between that fact, our problematic engine, and some traffic problems, we progressed very slowly. A few hours later we made it past Plymouth to the small hamlet of Bourbon, in which Arden Morris had grown up and where his parents still lived. He was confident that in the Bourbon/Plymouth area we would be able to undertake what by now we realized would be a quite extensive repair job on our vehicle's failing piston rings. No less  important, we could use his parents' home as a base while doing this, even though on arrival we learnt that they had left town and would not return until Tuesday. However, we had no difficulty being helped to settle in by several people known to Arden. My little diary entry for that day notes a "very friendly" visit with the parents of Arden's wife, Vivian, who were probably delighted to see their two young granddaughters, even though their own daughter had gone east with an earlier contingent. On that Sunday afternoon, we combined a bit of resting with starting to work on the repairs to the car, which continued into Monday, Tuesday, and well into Wednesday, before we got all the piston rings replaced and fine-tuned to our satisfaction. I say "our" satisfaction, but the truth is that I never was, nor wanted to be, a mechanic, though I was glad to help as much as I could. Pete and Arden, both more mechanically inclined and practical than I, took the lead. They also needed help from local mechanics, as they were also somewhat out of their depth. My diary entry for Monday, June 24, notes "Work repairing Cadillac. Learn more about V-8 engines than ever before. Man alive, what a time to " 'learn' "! With less frustration, it also notes the friendliness of the neighbors.

Arden's family belonged to the Church of the Brethren, and this area contained a considerable concentration of this Anabaptist sect. Indeed, his parents' absence when we first arrived was because they were away attending the Brethren Annual Conference. Though mostly working on the hearse, we also visited the nearby Brethren headquarters at Nappanee, where I continued my education on the variety of religious groups and their belief system that had settled or moved through the Midwest, for this was also Mennonite and Amish country.

Finally, on Thursday, June 27, the messy and tedious repairs completed, we were ready to continue eastward on Route 30 through Ohio and into Pennsylvania. By this point we were already well past the date we'd been expected at our destination, but we didn't realize the concern our absence had raised. A telephone connection had been made the night before, and I think there was both relief and annoyance from my dad, and Pete and Arden's spouses. The relief was in learning that we were in fact all right, and the annoyance that we had not managed to get a

message to them about what had happened and that it would be a couple more days before we would reach southeastern New York State.

In North Dakota, we never had to contend with heavy traffic, so this was my first real experience as a driver on heavily trafficked roads, and with traffic lights, but I quite quickly became accustomed to driving our hearse and mostly enjoyed it. It certainly provided a far smoother ride, as did the paved roads, than the trucks and tractors I had driven on our rutted North Dakota roads. Once we reached Pennsylvania, we got onto the limited access Pennsylvania Turnpike (toll road), which was a new experience, as was driving through heavily wooded hills. As night fell, we headed well off the main road to the home of a Bruderhof contact who awaited us. I cannot say I enjoyed driving in the twilight and then darkness along those winding roads, but we made it without mishap.

At our destination, as usual, I carried my sister Elizabeth, immobilized in her light body cast, into the house and to her bed. By now I was quite skilled at this task, and would probably not recall this instance, except that the attractive teenage daughter of the family expressed admiration for my skill and strength, which gave a glow of satisfaction to the rather scrawny teenage lad who accepted the compliment with whatever awkward gracefulness he could muster! My diary records neither the nearest town for this rural west central Pennsylvania home, nor the family's name beyond noting that they were somehow known or related to Arden and gave us a warm welcome.

Early the next morning on Friday, June 28, we set off on the last leg of the trip to the very temporary "Park Terrace Hotel" Bruderhof, just over the Pennsylvania border in New York State, between Fosterdale and Lake Huntingdon. It was the eighth day after our departure from Forest River. We arrived around 8:00 p.m. to join the main Forest River contingent, already well ensconced there. I had a quick supper and was shown the room I'd be sharing with my brother, Barnabas. Since it was still bright daylight, I was able to borrow the community's 1940 Buick and

take a couple of us down to the nearby lake to join other young folks there for a lovely and relaxing evening swim.

Next morning, Saturday, my first job was to mop the dining room floor. My diary notes cryptically, "Mop dining room floor. Ha ha!! First job here, last at Forest River!!"

Park Terrace proved to be an interesting fortnight-plus interlude. There was a small nearby Hasidic resort undergoing some refurbishment, and several of us were hired to assist with various jobs, with our earnings going directly to the Bruderhof, even though on paper this was my first paid labor. The pay was only minimum wage, I believe ninety-four cents per hour for nine-hour days, but it was interesting to me to interact with some of the folks there. My immediate boss was a pleasant enough lady, Abby, but the overall boss, Gene, who I think was her husband, was a bit of a taskmaster. Pleasanter were my interactions and discussions with two youngish, bearded rabbis (garbed outwardly not too differently from Hutterites!), last names Horowitz and Katz, whom I helped teach to drive. This endeavor was not entirely successful, as Rabbi Horowitz lost control of their little old Chevy "junky" while backing it down a grassy slope and knocked out a structural pillar of the little gazebo. Fortunately for me, I had warned him against the maneuver he was attempting, and the vehicle was not ours.

Disagreements with Gene, and someone named Joe, led to several Bruderhofers being let go. I was among the few retained into the following week. With the arrival of that Sabbath, I was introduced (mainly by Abby) to some of the ultraorthodox customs, including those pertaining to observant males not working on the Sabbath. But I, a goy/gentile, could be called to do some things, such as moving around the furniture. The curious *eretz* customs were also new to me, as were the types of devout prayer practices, particularly those performed by young men, who sported what to me were even stranger hairdos than the Hutterite cuts. Their Yiddish language was also remarkably like Hutterisch, no doubt due to the common geographic and Germanic linguistic roots of the shtetl and the Hutterite communes prior to their respective emigrations to North America. Yet another unexpected but fascinating addition to my education!

On the Fourth of July, I was introduced to a very different custom, as some of us visited the Independence Day fireworks at the nearby town. Here was something different to be savored — small town America, having noisy fun centered on an impressive fireworks display exceeding any I'd yet seen. Once again, very different from a Hutterite colony!

Early on Wednesday of the following week, since we were quite near the Woodcrest Bruderhof, a contingent of us left to visit there for the day and had a good time meeting up with old acquaintances. We arrived back quite late in the evening, and quite tired, for a late snack. Every night one of the men was assigned to be the night watch, to stay awake and ensure all remained secure and in good order. Though I had done night shifts on the farm tractors in Forest River, where we didn't have a formal night watch, I had never undertaken this duty here. I think Park Terrace instituted it in an excess of caution, in a new and unfamiliar place along a public highway. Anyway, on this night I was asked to do this job, and since it was already midnight, I agreed to do so as I had plenty of reading matter. It was a beautiful night with a full moon, and, both because of this and because getting up and walking around was a good way to fend off any sleepiness, I took several brief walks outside to gaze at the heavens and listen to the night sounds of the summer insects and birds of the rural northeastern United States region we now found ourselves in. Summer dawn came early. Before 6:00 a.m. a few people were starting to stir, and I began preparations for the communal breakfast, with others shortly joining in and taking over. I had been up for well over twenty-four hours, and by now was truly weary. I spent much of the rest of the day sleeping and feeling my first-time night watch responsibilities had been well dispatched.

Though the Bruderhof had closed on the Gorley Lake property in early June, they could not take possession until Monday, July 15, 1957. The

GORLEY'S LAKE HOTEL, UNIONTOWN, PA.

Altitude 2200 Feet   Always Cool   The Ideal Summer Reso

ALWAYS A FRIENDLY
WELCOME
GORLEY'S
LAKE HOTEL
In The Mountains
On U. S. Route 40
East of
UNIONTOWN, PA.
LAWRENCE ROSSI, Mgr.

decision was made that an advance contingent would get there on that date to clean the premises and prepare for the arrival of subsequent groups starting two days later. I was assigned to this advance party. We left Park Terrace on Sunday evening, July 14, driving overnight across Pennsylvania. We arrived in southwest Pennsylvania early on July 15 to prepare the old Gorley's Lake Hotel for the imminent arrival of the other Forest River emigrants at the new Oaklake Bruderhof, a lovely hilly and wooded location on the eastern side of the westernmost ridge of the Appalachians at 1,700 feet.

The evening before our vanguard group arrived the resort had had a final "going out of business" bash, and, upon our arrival, our first tasks included cleaning up from this event. This included savoring some of the leftovers, many unknown to us as they were rather "fancy" and too expensive for Bruderhof fare. I specifically recall the cold shrimp, and I think I hesitated to eat it, but more knowledgeable folks than I explained the "dip," and quickly I caught on to both shrimp and dip. Rather tasty!

Soon we moved from kitchen perishables cleanup to the more serious job of moving bed frames and mattresses to assigned rooms awaiting their new preassigned occupants, mostly in their family units. There were no elevators ("lifts" to me), so it was our manual labor that carted these metal frames, bedsprings, and mattresses from basement storage to the main family living quarters on the first and second floors. The third floor (formerly hotel staff quarters) contained mostly smaller, attic-type rooms, rather spartan in their furnishings, in which we set things up for unmarried adults. I fell into this category, and found myself sharing a bunk bed, much as I had in North Dakota, with my brother, Barnabas. Our room happened to be at the extreme eastern end of the corridor next to the fire escape exit. As a matter of convenience in the days to come, we often used these outside metal stairs to go down to the other floors and ground level rather than using the nicely carpeted broader indoor stairway. Quite safe though caution was certainly advised in inclement weather.

Quickly, we also turned to preparing for the start of Oaklake's Community Playthings manufacturing business, which would be very different from my previous exposures to the mostly agrarian underpinnings of my

Bruderhof life in Paraguay, England, and North Dakota. So, what was Community Playthings?

Rural settings and life on the land had dominated Bruderhof subsistence from its 1920s founding, though there had always been involvement in other enterprises, such as publishing and handicrafts, in both European and Paraguayan settings. As with the world around it, the Bruderhof was changing to more diversified enterprises. The establishment in 1954 of the first Bruderhof community in the United States, Woodcrest, saw a major shift in enterprise with the decision from the outset to engage in the manufacture of high-quality toys and equipment under the label of "Community Playthings" (CP). The business had actually started a little earlier in Georgia within the Macedonia community and under the name "Creative Playthings." But as a substantial proportion of the Macedonia membership joined Woodcrest, the business adjusted the name and shifted operations principally to Woodcrest. Community Playthings grew rapidly, adding a second manufacturing site at the second Bruderhof community, Evergreen (later Deerspring, located in western Connecticut).

By 1957, when Forest River was split, it was agreed that the new Oaklake community would also be integrated into the overall Community Playthings enterprise for the community's main economic base. Hence, very quickly after our arrival, both newcomers and more seasoned "CPers" brought in from Woodcrest, set up the workshop and machinery to take over parts of the overall Community Playthings manufacturing load, in full cooperation with Woodcrest, which was to remain the corporate headquarters and main manufacturer. There was general enthusiasm for this solution by the various brotherhoods, and at Oaklake, we went right to work. I was, naturally, part of this effort. Soon, though still small in size, Oaklake's shop (really, a little factory) was humming with activity. Most of the varied shop duties were done by males and involved various types of machinery for wooden toy manufacturing, along with preparing the incoming lumber (mostly maple), and then eventually shipping the assembled goods to their ultimate destinations. Some of the women were also involved, particularly in the fairly complex logistics of the whole process, and also in the preparation of the catalogues that described the products. Some of these catalogues also featured pictures of Bruderhof youngsters enjoying and testing new CP products, which indeed were of excellent quality!

Though all worked very hard in those first weeks, we did find ways to explore and enjoy our new surroundings. Unlike in northeastern North Dakota, we were now in the hills and valleys of southwestern Pennsylvania's coal country. The mines had already begun their long decline well before our 1957 arrival and this was overall an economically depressed area. I was surprised early on to find, right on our little property's surface, a vein of coal emerging from a slope just above our lake. Gorley's Lake was itself the product of the damming of a little valley creek to form a fourteen-acre lake (about to be renamed Oaklake), to provide the backdrop for this summer resort. The setting, with the main hotel building directly overlooking the lake, was lovely. The previous owners had constructed a little pier that also served as a little dock for several small aluminum rowboats that came with the sales package. The pier separated a shallow swimming area from the main lake, which was reserved for more experienced swimmers, as well as for those rowboats and for fishing.

It was quickly recognized that lake safety needed to be addressed, beyond the few signs regarding appropriate behavior in and near the water. Very soon, an experienced and credentialed swimming instructor, Mrs. Swaney, was hired to train some of us in lifeguard duties. As I later discovered, she was also an instructor at the Uniontown YMCA, which was located near our new community. We were eager pupils, not only because she was a good teacher, but maybe for some of the young males also because she brought along a young assistant, Ms. Arlene Jenkins, one of Mrs. Swaney's star swimmers in Uniontown, who was an extremely attractive teenager. Her swimming attire was somewhat more revealing than that of the Bruderhof young women. (I have wondered since what she may have thought of our group of trainees. Could we have seemed as unusual or strange to her as she was fascinating to some of us?).

Soon several of us received our credentials as certified lifeguards. We also obtained instruction on boating safety. Pool safety was generally not a problem for us guards in the highly disciplined world of the Bruderhof, but I think we all felt we benefitted from the instruction. I know I did.

This area of Pennsylvania was also very rich in United States history, as we soon learned. Within walking distance of Oaklake, for example, were the preserved remnants of Fort Necessity, where a young officer named

George Washington had been stationed with the British force under General Braddock, and where he began to make a name for himself well before he became the father of his country and the first president of the United States.

The move to Oaklake included a welcome development for me — the decision that I could return to complete high school, this time in the nearby Fayette County seat, Uniontown, to which my Bruderhof classmates and I were bused every day.

However, on January 26, 1958, scarcely six months after my arrival in Oaklake, and four months after returning to high school, I was told that arrangements had been made for me to move to a rooming house in Uniontown to complete my last year of high school from there. I was being expelled from the Bruderhof!

After my forced withdrawal from school in favor of farm labor at Forest River, I hardly expected to be expelled from the Bruderhof community for my academic interests and abilities. It was devastating.

Should I have anticipated this action? Though I'd realized my days at Oaklake were numbered, I hadn't known just how small that number was. At Uniontown High School I was making my mark academically. Indeed, though until then I'd never heard of the National Honor Society, my selection, along with my sister Joy's, was one of several irritants to some in the commune, which at that time harbored considerable ambivalence about academics. It certainly ranked such skills far lower than adherence to its increasingly evangelical and dogmatic religious outlook, and compliance with the often unstated and vague, but evidently important, norms of conduct which were at variance with my more liberal Wheathillian outlook. They had a point: even when I tried to, I really could not fit in comfortably with their values and found these trends away from the broader outreach of earlier European years to be very suffocating. However, I was quite unprepared to be cast out, in snowy January, with no local friends in Uniontown and no experience in integrating myself into that alien world.

The idea of my moving to Uniontown while finishing high school had been broached before January, but I'd argued for more time to consider my limited options. My hopes for a solution both the commune and I could

Welcome Back, Dr. Kovar!	**SENIOR HIGH NEWS** *Published by the students of the Senior High School of the Uniontown Joint High School System*	Support The Teams
Volume XXXIII	Thursday, January 23, 1958	Number 6

Students attaining high composite scores on the I.T.E.D. Tests are: seated, left to right—Anne Sauers, Carol Coughenour, Carl Marinacci, Neil Doppelt; standing—David Balling, Ben King, Tim Johnson.

agree on was perhaps unrealistic, and I may well have been in denial about my predicament regarding some in the Bruderhof leadership. Nonetheless, the suddenness of my leaving was a shock. On Saturday, January 25, I was summoned to a meeting with some of the Oaklake leadership and my parents. I knew it was serious, and by the end of the meeting, as my diary notes, I realized that they wanted me to leave Oaklake soon. I didn't feel ready and asked for more time, indicating that within a few weeks I might feel more open to their offer to allow me to complete high school while living in Uniontown with some support from the Bruderhof.

However, unbeknownst to me, arrangements had already been underway for my move and were confirmed to me the next day, Sunday, January 26. My parents had already met with the landlady at 229 Wilson Avenue, Miss Grace Reckner, and had arranged for a tiny rental room. She would provide me with a light breakfast each morning included in the room rental. The house was very close to Uniontown High School and on the same street.

After school the next day, Monday, Dad drove me from Oaklake with my baggage. He had a chat with me over coffee and pie before introducing me to my new room and landlady and helping me settle into my new digs. My diary confirms that I quite liked the room, but otherwise mainly notes that later in the evening "I studied," apparently settled into what was to be my temporary home until my high school graduation.

My removal from Oaklake was followed, within a few days, by my brother Barnabas's departure. Shortly after our arrival at Oaklake, the Bruderhof had established contact with Olney, a Friends (Quaker) boarding school near Barnesville, in southeast Ohio, a couple of hours' drive west from Oaklake. Barnabas seemed rather pleased when told that the Bruderhof had arranged with Olney to accept him into its freshman high school class, as he told me when he was allowed to stop briefly in Uniontown to say farewell as Dad drove him from Oaklake to his new home just a couple of days after my own Oaklake expulsion. In deference to his younger age, his promised to be a gentler transition to the outside world than mine, since the Quaker outlook on life was in several respects similar to the Bruderhof. In fact, I think the Bruderhof's decision for him was a win-win situation!"

Indeed, I would personally have welcomed a more gradual separation from the Bruderhof, especially with a group such as the Quakers, whose educational and general philosophy I felt more comfortable with than that of the mid-1950s Bruderhof. I'd tentatively raised such a general idea at Forest River after the positive experience more than a year earlier at the Iowa AFSC conference. At Oaklake, that was not given me as an option. A year later, my second sister, Susan, aged fourteen, was also "banished" to join Barnabas at Olney. Like Barnabas, she relished a move. It seems my parents' children were establishing a reputation for independence which misaligned with both the Bruderhof's stress on unity and conformity and what I will oversimplify as the North American communities' religious conservatism and Christian fundamentalism, at least in comparison with the European and Paraguayan communities, combined with continuing engagement with the Hutterites. Understandably and painfully, this reputation also contributed to an already stressful situation for our parents.

In the next weeks after my arrival in Uniontown, several things happened. First, the academic interests which were such a stumbling block in the commune had the opposite effect at the high school. Such things as very high scores on national standardized exams, a nomination for a DAR American History award (withdrawn when my United Kingdom citizenship was belatedly noted), and two articles, with my picture, in the school newspaper, helped me develop a circle of friends at school. The fact that I did not spend time with the other Bruderhof children and my non-United States background made me a bit of a mystery!

Second, I managed to get by despite very little money for the basic necessities from the Bruderhof. My work as a dishwasher in the school cafeteria qualified me for lunch. My usual dinner was an inexpensive hamburger and mini salad at a local diner called Joe's. I was welcomed at the public library and worked for a membership at the YMCA, where I could swim. Joy, who was in homeroom with me, took home my laundry and kept me informed of things happening at Oaklake, as did my dad on his occasional visits.

Third, I benefitted greatly in finding my way with the assistance of a few "angels."

The Uniontown High School principal, Dr. Dan Kovar, took an interest in me when he became aware I no longer lived at the commune. Soon, he helped launch me toward the higher educational aspirations I had barely allowed myself to dream about.

My other angels were Pierce and Liza Gault, a couple who visited Oaklake from Washington, DC, at Easter, 1958, after my expulsion. Their visit coincided with my first return to Oaklake since my January departure. By the end of a long conversation, from which they gathered that not only was I unlikely to return permanently to the commune, but also that I had no prospects beyond high school, they gave me their contact information in Washington, DC, and told me to look them up if I found myself there. None of us realized then how much they were destined to help me in coming months!

SCHISMS

Summer, 1958
Oaklake Bruderhof to Washington, DC

Peyton Place

*Tim and Joy, Uniontown
High School graduates, June 1958*

In June 1958, I graduated from Uniontown High School a year later than I would have without the interruptions to my schooling in England and North Dakota. I now had a high school diploma, but no job and few prospects. The Bruderhof had agreed in May to lend me a small sum to enable me to hitchhike to Pittsburgh for an intense extended weekend of submitting job applications. With the strong encouragement of Dr. Kovar, I'd also submitted a few applications for college admissions and financial assistance and interviewed at the University of Pittsburgh as part of their application process. While I waited for any of these efforts to bear fruit, the Bruderhof agreed that I could return to Oaklake briefly after graduation and work in the Community Playthings workshop in exchange for room and board.

While waiting for the bus that would take me up the mountain to Oaklake, I picked up a paperback copy of a current bestseller, which I'd seen other

Uniontown High School students reading and I knew to be controversial. The "other students" included two young women and one lad from the Bruderhof who were all still living there. Though they rode the school bus between school and the Bruderhof, they apparently didn't travel with the book. How they'd obtained it I never asked, but sensed they chose only to read it "off-hof," perhaps keeping it in their school lockers. It was, for me, a "don't ask, don't tell" situation.

I never suspected it could be so toxic to have it in my possession. I don't remember thinking much about it as I read a few pages before catching the eastbound Greyhound bus as darkness fell. *Peyton Place* was clearly a bit racy by contemporary 1950s standards, and even more so by Bruderhof standards, so I realized it would probably be best not to be too obvious in reading it at Oaklake.

As it turned out, I never got the chance to read it there. The space I was assigned to as my temporary quarters was rather public, as it was on the top floor and adjacent to the metal fire escape on the outside of the main building. (It was the most direct way for those of us housed there to go down to the dining hall and outside.) There, I bedded down with my few belongings, including a few books, none of which I tried to hide. One of them was my bus stop *Peyton Place* purchase, still essentially unread by me. While I was there, I had a number of drop-by visits by people I knew well who just wished to hang out and talk. One was a Bruderhof high school student a couple of years younger than me named Dave, who had started reading the book at Uniontown but not completed it. He saw my copy and decided to finish reading it. His conscience rather belatedly apparently kicked in then.

I am no longer clear on the exact sequence of the rather fast-moving events after that, but Dave reported his "transgression" both to me and another young man, John. Somehow, they decided the book should be burnt.

That evening, while most adult members were in a routine meeting, Dave and John, with me in attendance, held a little ceremony of burning my fifty-cent book, which went up in flames just beyond the car park area of the community. I argued against this action, but evidently not convincingly enough. It probably didn't help that, like John, I was treating this "ritual" as a bit of a joke, though Dave took it more seriously. Around this point, and still unknown to me (and perhaps it didn't happen until the next morning) Dave had also felt the need to confess to one of the lead brothers that he'd transgressed in his reading, which inevitably led to further questions about how he'd come to have the book. That inquisition quickly and directly led to me.

That afternoon, while at work at Community Playthings, I was summoned to a meeting of the senior brothers. Other than explaining that I'd not yet read the book, and the circumstances of my having it at all, I recall little of the meeting. I thought I'd made clear what I felt was my quite peripheral role in the matter. I returned to my place on the assembly line, but not for long. Soon, I was informed that someone would take my place on the line. It was left to my dad to tell me that right after I'd been dismissed from the earlier meeting, those senior brothers quickly decided I must leave the community immediately, though it was already late afternoon, and almost the end of the working day.

I pleaded to stay the night and leave the next morning, but those pleadings fell on deaf ears. Instead, I was lent fifty dollars to hitchhike away, right after an early solitary supper and a quick shower after my day's labor. My mother was in tears, my father ashen faced as he told me the decision and drove me a few miles east on United States Route 40, formerly known as the "National Road." My first ride picked me up just as daylight was fading. Not knowing where to go, but since the vehicle was headed east, that's where I went.

Several hours, several rides, and one thunderstorm later and no longer on Route 40, I was dropped off at a landmark I well recognized though I'd never been there. I was in Washington, DC, at the foot of the Washington Monument, and it was very early  morning. I was hungry, but even more tired. A park bench beckoned me to a fitful sleep.

I've mentioned my "angels," Pierce and Liza Gault. In the next days, I contacted them, and their home became my base as I pounded the streets of Washington in search of work, eventually landing a position as a bookstore clerk. They became not just friends, but wise counselors, helping this naïve and inexperienced teenage lad navigate a world that was new, sometimes alien, yet also fascinating. They were even indirect pointers to the job I secured as a salesclerk at a branch of Brentano's Book Store across from the National Zoo. The only way they allowed me to repay them was to be a companion to Liza's octogenarian mother, a delight in her own right, for a few weeks while Pierce, Liza, and their teenage daughter, Sally, served as counselor/managers for a young people's retreat a few hours away in Virginia.

Once I had a job, I wrote to my parents with contact information. My dad soon phoned, his voice full of relief that I was okay after the distressing circumstances of my departure. He also passed along some interesting news: I'd been accepted for that fall's classes, with a full tuition scholarship, at the University of Pittsburgh. Should I accept it, knowing I had still almost no savings toward lodging and meals? Or should I accept Brentano's offer that if I'd stay a full year before heading for college, they'd upgrade my title to "assistant branch manager" and, more importantly, raise my pay somewhat above my starting minimum wage level? Perhaps for the first time in my life, I had two promising options to consider.

Several decades later I found myself taking a summer-evening stroll from my Washington hotel, and back once more to the grounds of the Washington Monument. Once again, I lay on a hard bench, and then on the soft grass, and contemplated with satisfaction the intervening years, and how my fortunes had changed, from the sense of betrayal I had felt in 1958 to the sense of accomplishment that I now felt in a life well lived. A life that in some senses was launched that mild yet bitter night in early June 1958.

Fall, 1958
University of Pittsburgh
An Unapologetic Life of the Mind

I couldn't take too much time that summer of 1958 to consider those two positive choices presented to me — accept the full tuition scholarship offer from the University of Pittsburgh (Pitt) to continue my education or accept the offer from Brentano's to spend the next year in DC working for a higher hourly pay rate and a promotion. After all, both entities needed a decision from me! After thoughtful consideration, I chose to accept the offer from Pitt. It was a welcome "bird in the hand" next step for me in a direction I only hoped and dreamed of — an unapologetic life of my mind no less than my hands.

I contacted a Uniontown friend, Bennett Friedman, who I knew was planning to attend Pitt. He invited me to share a small and inexpensive apartment with him and another former Uniontown student, Bill Tantlinger, who was a sophomore at the nearby Carnegie Institute of Technology (later, Carnegie Mellon University), as there was no way I could afford a dorm room. In September 1958, I started my undergraduate studies while simultaneously covering (barely!) my room and living expenses with a part-time minimum wage custodial job at the university.

After a few months, Bill transferred to the University of West Virginia and Bennett decided to move to a campus fraternity house. It was clear I would need to find other lodgings as I did not have enough money for dormitory living. However, during the Christmas holiday period (I think just into January 1959, actually), I got a surprise call from Dad to tell me that he and Mother would be passing through Pittsburgh and asking whether it would be possible for them to stay with me for a day or two. Since neither of my roommates would be there, the arrangement would work, though my parents' timing seemed strange to me.

Winter, 1958-1959
University of Pittsburgh, Cleveland, Oaklake
Ausschluss!

When my parents arrived, they told me that they had been placed in "*ausschluss*," to use the common Germanic term favored by the Bruderhof for exclusion, and would temporarily be moving to Cleveland, Ohio, where Dad would be doing some work for the Bruderhof and where he had some contacts. They did not go into great detail, and I felt it best not to ask too many questions, but I gathered there was another crisis brewing at the community, though whether just at Oaklake or something bigger I did not know at the time. While my parents were sent away for "consideration," their younger children remained at Oaklake. Our parents hoped soon to be able to return to the community and their family.

Since Dad had a Bruderhof car with him, we took the opportunity to drive a bit around the neighborhood. We located a tiny inexpensive room in a small rooming house about a mile on the other side of the Pitt campus near the Magee-Womens Hospital, and I made an immediate move with my few belongings. My parents then continued to Cleveland and their efforts to find their way back to the Bruderhof and their fractured family.

I no longer recall just how many months our parents were gone from Oaklake, but with the Bruderhof's permission I did manage to hitchhike the sixty miles from Pittsburgh to Oaklake on a few Saturday afternoons, leaving after work and staying overnight to Sunday afternoon, mainly so that I could look in on my younger sisters, who (given that I'd been gone most of the previous year) didn't really seem to know who I was, or at least knew only rather vaguely. At least one of them seemed quite upset at her parents' sudden and unexplained departure, and though assured that they would be back, remained unconvinced. Indeed, it turned out she wasn't sure whether to believe that they were even still alive. Based on a conversation with her about this many years later, my insistence to her at that time that they were quite alive, and I'd seen them (in Pittsburgh), still did not fully reassure her. Such were the cruelties inflicted on children by the "church discipline" endured by their parents!

Summer, 1959
Oaklake, Woodcrest
My Best Time at a Bruderhof

Within a few months, my parents were allowed to return to Oaklake and briefly things seemed to be better. Indeed, I was able to arrange with Hardi Arnold, serving as the servant at Oaklake, and Howard Johnson (no relative of my parents), the community's steward, or financial officer, at Oaklake, that I could spend the 1959 summer vacation period there with my family while working in the Community Playthings workshop. Hardi and I had gotten on quite well at Forest River when he was the servant there. The previous year, he'd shown some understanding of my academic interests and had even given me the gift of a little paperback philosophy book while treating me to a beer, so I felt secure in this plan. In Pittsburgh, I arranged that I could have my room back after the summer, and could meanwhile leave my belongings there, though my landlady could temporarily rent the room to someone else in my absence, as I had only put down a deposit to guarantee my September return.

It sounded like a win-win — I'd be with my family and the Bruderhof would have cheap labor. But, again, another Bruderhof crisis was underway and would have to be navigated. Shortly after my arrival at Oaklake, I was given a strange two-part message. First, I was told that if I saw Hardi Arnold around, I should avoid speaking to him. He had been placed in *ausschluss*. Second, since there were problems at this community, they would prefer me not to stay for the summer as they were sorting out this crisis.

Now what? I had given up my room in Pittsburgh and my part-time university job for the summer. I remonstrated that I had neither prospects nor money and had taken the community's offer in good faith. For once, a compromise was suggested. I could not stay at Oaklake, so I would not be with my family. However, I could hitchhike to the Woodcrest community in New York State, work in the shop there, and participate in community activities. I would be unpaid, like all members, but would have room and board. I agreed, and was given ten dollars to hitchhike to New York, where I spent a rather enjoyable summer living with several other young men (I was the youngest) in a place known, for rather self-explanatory reasons, as the "bughouse." It was quite convenient as it was in the woods very near the Community Playthings factory where I spent most working days. It was also very close to the Wallkill River, with its nearby scenic covered bridge, and was maybe a five- to ten-minute walk to the main buildings complex, which included the dining and meeting rooms. As a nice bonus for me, since staying with my parents and younger siblings had been canceled, my sister Joy had been moved to Woodcrest, so I had at least one family member I could talk to (though both she and I were advised not to be seen as being too close.)

In retrospect, this two-month period at Woodcrest in the summer of 1959, starting more than a year after my expulsion, was probably the best time I had at any Bruderhof in North America. No one put pressure on me to join, yet I was allowed to be actively involved in the youth group and enjoyed meeting with other young visitors. At the end of the summer, I hitchhiked back to Oaklake, where I was able to stay for a few days with my family before returning to Pittsburgh and reclaiming my room. This phase of the Oaklake crisis was over, but it only turned out to be the calm before the next big storm for the commune.

Christmas 1959 to Spring 1961
Oaklake to Cleveland
My Parents' Expulsion

T he calm remained through Christmas, 1959, when the rest of my siblings and I were able to celebrate the season with our parents at Oaklake. We enjoyed our family time together, though we surmised it might also be the last time so many of us would be together. At Oaklake, we were already getting intimations of the major changes ahead for all Bruderhofs in the coming two

The Johnsons – Eleanor, Guy, Rosie, Rebecca, Elfie, Elizabeth – at Oak Lake, February 1961

years, first in the leadership of most of the communes (other than Woodcrest, where Elder Heini Arnold held undisputed sway), then for the very existence of the South American communities, and then for Wheathill.

But before that, and reflecting some of the currents underlying these upheavals, the Johnson family found itself unceremoniously banished from Oaklake by the new regime. It happened in March 1961. My parents were given an aging Plymouth and two hundred dollars to drive away with their four youngest children (and the pet hamster). They headed for Cleveland, which was somewhat known to them from their earlier temporary exclusion.

My parents' expulsion in 1961 was at the leading edge of what was to be the end of the Bruderhof as we, and many other first- and second-generation Bruderhofers, had known it. In the next two years, with the closing of most of the existing communities, well over half of the

Guy with Plymouth and family in Cleveland, August 1961

pre-1950s families were either expelled or, in a few cases, left voluntarily. In all cases, those who left (referred to as "the Leavers") had to start over with virtually no resources, often in countries they were unfamiliar with and often with large families headed by parents with few marketable skills and rarely with references and contacts to help them find employment.

Compared to many others, our family coped and survived relatively well.

Barnabas, Susan, and I had all left by early 1961, and it turned out that Joy also left the same year. After leaving Oaklake in November 1958 and enduring a rather painful period at two of the American communes, followed by a brief period at the new Bulstrode community that had replaced Wheathill in England, she too had left to start her nursing career.

So ended our parents' twenty-two years of faithful service to their ideals and beliefs, or at least their efforts to realize them through a Christian "community of goods."

PART TWO - MY OWN JOURNEY

Chapter 7 – 1958-1961
University of Pittsburgh, BSc

Die Gedanken sind Frei!

My undergraduate years were a time of intellectual growth and freedom. The monetary strictures notwithstanding, I was free to pursue intellectual discovery — exploring several lines of possible academic specialization and becoming involved in social, athletic,

and political activities, particularly after my first two years and into my initial post-graduate period. These were the early years of the Vietnam War and of the civil rights struggles, particularly in the southern United States but with strong ripples across the northern universities, including Pitt. I was a student member and then officer of several groups, including the Young People's Socialist League (YPSL) and the Student Peace Union (SPU). I was also involved with local Friends (Quakers) and attended their meetings fairly regularly for some years. This

period included John F. Kennedy and Hubert Humphrey battling for the Democratic presidential nomination in 1960, when both visited our campus, as did the old socialist stalwart, and a personal hero for me, Norman Thomas. Somewhat later, I had the privilege of introducing Michael Harrington, author of *The Other America,* to a packed campus meeting hall in Pitt's Cathedral of Learning.

These years were also unfortunately a time of considerable financial hardship for me, yet somehow, I scraped by. I necessarily lived a very hand-to-mouth life of extreme frugality, with my part-time job at barely minimum wage. Early on, I discovered a Goodwill store and would walk there for cheap necessities, including used but serviceable clothes and footwear and a few eating utensils.

I liked sports and was becoming a fan of American popular sports like baseball. My poverty didn't keep me from following Pittsburgh Pirates baseball on the radio or from very occasionally seeing them play, as their field was part of the campus. Roberto Clemente was a favorite player of mine due to his on-field finesse and off-field humanitarianism, which unfortunately was the cause of the early end to his life.

At the rooming house on Halket Street, I briefly had a roommate (although not from Pitt) whose study habits were not at all compatible with mine. Fortunately, a single room soon became available, and, for peace of mind, I took it despite the strain on budget from the additional couple of dollars' rent per week.

I shared a bathroom with several others. My furniture consisted of my bed, a little writing desk that also served as my dining space, and a chair. I'd pick up a few food items, mostly avoiding perishables, except for bread and milk, from a grocery store between the university and my lodging. I had a shelf where I could store a few canned goods (soups, tinned fish), plus margarine, peanut butter and jam, sliced bread (sometimes day-old surplus), boxed cereal, and a few eggs I could boil. These were my staples. Stops at Goodwill also yielded such necessities as a teapot and saucepan along with a small electric hot plate on which I could heat water for the teapot. A couple of dollars got me a serviceable little AM radio, good for keeping up with world news and a bit of music. In the colder months, my windowsill sometimes would provide a little "refrigeration." Dishwashing was done in rather rudimentary fashion in the bathroom sink.

My part-time duties at the university came in handy in several respects beyond simply giving me a paycheck. First, in common with the other young custodial employees, my hours were somewhat flexible as there was an understanding with our two full-time university staff supervisors that our first priority had to be our studies. In my case, and very kindly, one of these bosses would some days, by prearrangement, bring in a second sandwich along with his own, for which he charged me at a very low rate. Certainly, better fare than what I could make in my room at the rooming house! Furthermore, we student employees had access to a common locker room area in the catacombs of the Cathedral of Learning where we could store such things as our course materials (books) and changes of clothes and take after-work showers. I often took my showers there before returning to my own quarters.

A different yet equally helpful aspect of my work was that on a few occasions some of the secretaries (as they were known then) in administrative offices where I would make my cleanup rounds realized my strained economic circumstance and kindly offered to take my handwritten term papers and type them up for me. This gesture was something I particularly appreciated, as I had no typewriter and some assignments required typed submissions. In some ways, I think the people I met through my job also served as something of a social outlet for me. Anyway, I was very grateful to them!

I was well aware that my diet was nutritionally inadequate during this time, but I sensed that the way to get beyond the poverty hurdle was to advance my education enough to allow me to improve my socio-economic status beyond that which my part-time work afforded. If I had to forego pleasures others could enjoy to maintain my scholarship, so be it. From my earlier Bruderhof life, I'd learned to keep my expectations quite low, and I also think in some ways my early Bruderhof coping skills helped during those years, along with finding ways simply to scramble as best I could to stay afloat. Beggars can't be choosers, and often I had to scrimp, but I was also fortunate that during that period I suffered no major illnesses or other misfortunes sufficient to derail me. And slowly, I worked myself into a better economic situation once I gained the academic credentials to get a somewhat better paying part-time hospital microbiology laboratory position.

Besides my major in bacteriology, my undergraduate studies included strong concentrations in chemistry and physics. However, I also managed to satisfy a growing interest in the humanities and social sciences with coursework concentrations in English and geography, along with a grab bag of miscellaneous courses, including my first smatterings of statistics, economics, and demography, as I tried to define and refine my career interests.

Though I could perhaps not have articulated this at the time, I was gravitating toward both public health and human population studies and combining these with my international interests. Indirectly, my earlier experiences in the Bruderhof and with the Hutterites undoubtedly influenced these directions. I was raised among the first generation of Bruderhofers, who had been characterized by a strong social concern with issues of poverty and inequities during that period of economic depression as an impetus to their religious outreach orientation. Circumstances beyond my control had already taken me to impoverished rural areas of Paraguay, as well as England, followed by my North Dakota period when I was a teenager.

When our family moved to North Dakota, I was personally fascinated by the Hutterites' remarkably large family sizes. When my parents arrived at Forest River with their eight children, we took over what had until recently been the home of the even larger family of Paul Maendel, who had returned to Manitoba. Next to our prairie home was the house occupied by Joe and Mary Maendel, parents of fifteen living children, though the oldest of these were already establishing their own families in separate quarters. On our other side were Allan and Edna Baer, with ten children under the age of fourteen (and with more to come). While Bruderhof families tended to be large by western standards, as ours was with its eight children, they were no match for the Hutterite fertility rates, which I was later to learn were the closest approximation demographers could find to theoretical natural human fertility limits anywhere on Earth. At that time, and only based on their exceptional natural reproduction rates, Hutterite colonies typically doubled about every sixteen years. Were these doubling rates going to be sustainable, in the long run, even in the seemingly endless open spaces of the United States and Canadian west? Others were already asking such questions and seeking answers, though this was not yet my focus.

From an intellectual standpoint, I would also go back in my mind to my initial introduction, while I was a student at Wheathill, to Thomas Malthus and his first essay on the relationship between population and poverty. His thesis was that pressures of population growth pitted against limited agricultural growth capacity would inevitably doom efforts to improve the lot of the working classes. Our young headmaster and principal teacher, Derek Wardle, had no sympathy for this view, and approvingly quoted Karl Marx, some decades after Malthus, railing about Pastor Malthus as a "sycophant of the ruling classes." Much as I liked Derek, then and later, I felt that maybe there was more to Malthus's thesis than Derek's simple dismissal of Malthus's arguments and his "dismal science" of economics deserved. Were there other factors beyond inequities of distribution created by capitalism that needed to be addressed in discussions of the Great Depression of the 1930s or the devastation of the great Irish potato famine? We knew of both situations as historical events, but not their causes, nor how the balance of population and resources figured into these disasters. They certainly seemed to illustrate Malthus's principle in very stark terms. I did not pursue it and the more sophisticated and nuanced arguments of both sides until years later in college. Yet, it had stuck with me, particularly when I later lived among the Hutterites and began to see other aspects of rapid population growth in a finite world.

This would be grist for later study, but meanwhile my own observations of population in relation to resources were among factors that within a few years helped launch me into a career in population and reproductive health, albeit more in developing country settings than in rural America.

CHAPTER 8 - 1962-1966

University of Pittsburgh, MSc

Launching My Career (But Not Smoothly)

I completed my undergraduate studies for my bachelor's degree in December 1961. At that time, I was accepted for doctoral studies by Pitt's bacteriology program, and provided with a teaching and research assistant (TA/RA) position in bacteriology, to commence after graduation. My initial thinking was that I'd proceed to a PhD in bacteriology or would switch to medical school and aim for an MD, as I was accepted into both programs. Though I embarked on both tracks, a combination of personal and financial circumstances soon derailed these options, and by mid-1963 I found myself out of school, deep in debt, and unemployed.

Fortunately, this unemployment lasted only a few weeks. Soon I began working full-time as a laboratory technician at UPMC Presbyterian hospital and part-time as a general medical technician at an adjacent hospital (eye and ear). By mid-1964, while still working full-time and more, I had redirected my studies and was taking courses in the Graduate School of Public and International Affairs (GSPIA), and through the Graduate School of Public Health. Initially, I could only

Tim, as a University of Pittsburgh graduate student, June 1966

afford the time and tuition fees for part-time graduate study. However, by mid-1965, and aided by a public health fellowship, I was able to reduce my hospital work to part-time responsibilities while studying full-time. My focus had meanwhile become much better defined within the field of international public health, with an emphasis on international population and family planning work. This, I'd become convinced, was not only an extremely important though much neglected field, but one that also presented intellectual and practical challenges I was eager to explore and was consistent with my own evolving personal philosophy.

As an aside, my parents, having eight children, were somewhat bemused by my "population" interest, but accepted my choices and reasoning. They had returned with their remaining children to England after being expelled from the commune. I only saw them once between 1961 and 1968, and our relations improved once they were permanently out of the Bruderhof. However, it was only many years later that my mother told me that as a socially and politically progressive young woman she had actually supported the birth control league activities of the 1930s in England but had avoided the subject in the strongly pronatalist and anti-family planning Bruderhof and Hutterite years that followed.

Elizabeth, Tim, and Rip, on a visit to England, summer 1964

Since no formal population planning academic concentration existed yet anywhere at Pitt, I started to design my own program, anchored in the School of Public Health, but with courses handpicked from international affairs, economics, and sociology in addition to public health. By good fortune, the associate dean of the public health school, Dr. Sam Wishik, had just returned from a sabbatical in Pakistan, where he was involved in the early stages of their national family planning program.[1] Soon, he became my academic advisor, my mentor, and later also a good friend. After discussions with him and others in the School of Public Health, I opted to follow the Master of Science (MSc) rather than the Master of Public Health (MPH) degree track. It allowed for a somewhat more customized course of studies and had a few formal requirements beyond the MPH coursework. Among these was to conduct and write a research-based study in the general field of maternal and child health and family-planning. As was true for my public health coursework, the study went well, and as far as my committee and I were aware, all requirements had been met for me to receive my diploma in June 1966.

The Friday evening preceding formal graduation ceremonies, and blissfully unaware there might be a problem, I visited the public health school where I'd just been offered an interesting research position for the next months and was met with the urgent message that my advisor, Dr. Sam Wishik, had been trying to reach me. I promptly spoke with him and learned that an important final formal requirement had yet to be fulfilled: a faculty committee needed to certify that I'd taken and passed both a final written and oral comprehensive Master of Science exam. This certification needed to be completed before my formal graduation date on the coming Monday or my graduation would be delayed. I think we'd all been unaware of this requirement because no such comprehensive exam was required for the MPH degree. As it was, Dr. Wishik had already been made aware of the problem, so when I reached him he'd already discussed how best to resolve this requirement with other faculty members.

He told me I still had the weekend to study, and the three-member committee who would examine me had been contacted to schedule both parts of the exam. He would chair the committee. Fortunately, I had taken courses with the other two. I had very limited review time in those next two days and took the good advice to look back at whatever notes I had from those two professors, especially for the oral component, which

---

[1] My work with Dr. Wishik, beginning in 1966, included the initial development of the CYP Index, an aggregate measure of protection against unwanted or mistimed pregnancies provided by all contraceptive methods available through a family planning program. More about the CYP Index and my role in its development and use is in the appendix E.

(because of the limited time) would be quite early on Monday morning, allowing time for the written part, which would then have to be assessed. Could I do it? I didn't have time to panic.

By the time my orals were done, I felt quite good about how they'd gone. Then, straight into the written part, with the clock and my adrenaline both running. I felt pretty good about my responses, but once finished, I could only wait for the results. In some respects, some of the questions seemed almost tailor-made for me, which may have reflected that the committee members knew my international interests and hopes for the future along with my academic record. Yet, until that signed document was formally submitted, I was on tenterhooks. At one point, I asked Dr. Wishik's secretary when she thought the committee might complete its work. She knew I was concerned but could officially say nothing. She did, however, offer an important clue — that she'd seen Dr. Wishik chuckle when reading my response to one of the essay questions. A good sign!

And so it was that Monday afternoon I did indeed find myself, with cap and gown, joining my fellow Graduate School of Public Health's master's degree recipients!

I received my MSc degree, and in anticipation, began to look for an overseas posting in which I could apply what I'd learnt, and could perhaps also start working toward a doctorate in population studies. Three possibilities emerged, but while I explored these, I needed a full-time job!

My statistics professor, Isidor Altman, in whose course I'd excelled and who knew of my emerging career interests, invited me to work for him as chief field officer in a project he headed under President Lyndon Johnson's new Great Society health program. Between June and October, my job was to use my little Honda motorcycle to collect health statistics from a large number of health facilities in four southwest Pennsylvania counties (Fayette, Washington, Greene, and Westmoreland) and to help analyze these statistics to identify underserved areas. Already familiar with these areas from my Uniontown residency (Fayette County) and having briefly visited rural Kentucky and studied some of the health issues in this "Other America," I was delighted by this invitation to work with Professor Altman and his little staff, which I did until early October.

A. Richey Sharrett, Naomi Lau, and I were welcomed overnight by this family in Leslie County, KY. They were part of Richey's previous summer's health and poverty in Appalachia research.

By then, with my principal interest in global population problems, I'd accepted a posting with the Ford Foundation's Pakistan office to assist their population officer in Karachi, Dr. Ralph Sachs, in the foundation's work with the new national family planning program. I was ready to head for Pakistan, with my choice no doubt influenced by Dr. Wishik, through whom I'd already familiarized myself with some of the myriad issues facing that country and its population. By early October 1966, arrangements were in place for me to embark on my first overseas professional assignment and a new chapter in my life.

CHAPTER 9 - CITIZENSHIP

A Noteworthy Detour – My United States Citizenship Challenges

Before my story heads off to Pakistan, I wish to detour back a few years to describe the evolution of my personal philosophy. The religious but quite socially active commune I'd been raised in, both in England and Paraguay, was strongly anti-war as well as very international in its membership. In this, the Bruderhof reflected the pacifist leanings of such traditional "peace churches" as the Society of Friends, and the Anabaptist Mennonite and Hutterite Christian denominations, which in part inspired some of its members. I was raised without strongly nationalist sentiments, which actually were discouraged as the search for harmony and unity was a guiding principle, and since we enjoyed the music, folk dancing, and games from several cultures.

Just as I'd rather assumed as a youngster that I would eventually join the Bruderhof commune, I also assumed I'd adopt the religious and social values of the only society I'd really known. My assumption began to change as I entered my teens and began (as teens often do) to question the basis for my inherited beliefs, especially as I became a bit more familiar with what was referred to as "the outside world." For the first time, I suppose, I also wondered whether the Bruderhof's straight and narrow path would forever be my own.

In both the United States and United Kingdom, young males were required to register for the draft and potential conscription into military service. I knew that at some point I'd face the decision whether I would serve, or whether I would choose to be a conscientious objector to war. Military service would be anathema to the Bruderhof, and if I joined the community, I could expect their support in seeking alternative service.

However, though I supported most of the social message of the Bruderhof, including avoidance of military solutions to national and international disputes, I was increasingly at odds with their religious beliefs and demands.

Under the operative laws in both the United Kingdom and the United States, to which I was destined soon to emigrate, belonging to a religion with a pacifist tradition was a virtual requirement for gaining conscientious objector (CO) status. This, I could already foresee, could become a major problem for me.

By virtue of a decision by the Bruderhof, it was decided our family would leave England to help with the establishment of communes in North America. We left England on my sixteenth birthday, so I had a couple of years ahead of me before registering for the draft at eighteen. I did so in high school in Uniontown, Pennsylvania. By then, however, it was clear that my personal path was moving inexorably further from the Bruderhof.

As a noncitizen and a green-card resident alien, I guess I thought I might not be drafted, but this was not the case. Fortunately, I also learned that I would not have to declare my wish to be a conscientious objector until required to by the local draft board, and that while I was a university undergraduate, it was unlikely I'd be called up. College deferment bought me some time to try to sort out my own concerns about future decisions. Yet eventually these would have to be faced.

Meanwhile, as an undergraduate at Pitt, I continued to develop my own values. I sometimes attended the local Quaker meeting, though neither as a full member nor a believer in any of the more overtly religious aspects, yet I was strongly attracted to their humanistic philosophy. Concurrently, the late 1950s were transitioning into the turbulent 1960s, in ways few could yet see.

In late 1960, I was much taken by the dynamic young senator, John F. Kennedy, including his call for a form of voluntary national service, the Peace Corps. That was something I could in good conscience serve in! Or so I thought. With graduation nearing and with Kennedy now president, I stopped at a Peace Corps recruiting station at the student union to check on this as an option.

My British accent prompted the recruiter's question, "Are you an American citizen?" Oops! I guess I'd naively thought that, since I'd already been in the United States for some years, was quite active on campus, and had registered for the military draft, as required, citizenship was not an urgent matter. Not so, I discovered, to serve in the Peace Corps.

This situation was among various factors leading to my decision to seek citizenship. However, here I encountered a bit of a Catch-22, though Joseph Heller had not yet coined that Kafkaesque phrase. Citizenship required an oath of allegiance, including the willingness to bear arms. Yet, though still not formally cleared by my draft board as a CO, I knew I was definitely a pacifist, though my basis was more political and ethical than religious.

In 1963, I decided to apply to the Immigration and Naturalization Service (INS) to become a citizen. I submitted all the necessary paperwork and was scheduled for an INS appointment. I was confident I'd have no difficulty with the American history part. After all, at Uniontown High, I'd been nominated for an Americanism award. True, it was withdrawn once the sponsors of the award, the DAR, discovered the high scorer in the United States history course was not a United States citizen!

Possibly this situation was a harbinger of what happened next, as the INS grilled me on my earlier student activities, which had included membership in several somewhat left-leaning political groups. All my activities had been consistent with my strongly held views that violence was not the answer to the world's, or our country's, problems. However, they were not rooted in religiously based objections to bearing arms. The upshot was that my citizenship petition was denied. Now what? INS told me I could appeal the decision, but at that point I had no financial resources to do so, and since the decision did not affect my current resident alien status, I simply licked my wounds and continued with work and graduate studies, knowing I could revisit the citizenship question when my personal circumstances allowed.

About two years after my initial citizenship denial, I was able to resolve my draft status, in part due to a decision by the United States Supreme Court. In this early 1965 case, a political/ethical basis for refusal to bear arms was granted (United States v. Seeger). It was among the arguments I brought to my draft board regarding my own case. In brief, my draft status was eventually resolved, and I was granted conscientious objector status. It would still require noncombatant service once I was drafted. I was fine with that decision, and with receiving 1-A-O status stamped on my induction papers when I was called for my preinduction physical. Having nothing as serious as "bone spurs" as excuses to fail the physical, I was declared fit to serve. But doing what, and where, and would I even be called up, and what would be the nature of my alternate service? And what about the citizenship issue, left in limbo two years earlier?

Now that my draft board had upheld my reasoning for being granted noncombatant status, perhaps it was time to revisit the citizenship issue. After all, despite my opposition to the Vietnam War, I had not changed my mind about wishing to become an American. Also, in the two years since the initial decision, I'd managed to get on better financial footing and I decided to appeal the earlier denial.

I really had no legal access, nor substantial monetary resources, but a young Black lawyer, David Washington, whom I'd known as an undergraduate when he was a law student, agreed to represent me in my appeal. I collected documents related to my case and he obtained the transcripts from my initial hearings (when I'd had to waive legal counsel), and together we presented my case in late 1965. He was deeply involved in civil rights issues and he knew my interest from our earlier contact. He used this background to help make my case.

We won! On December 10, 1965, about ten years after I first arrived in the United States, and standing before federal district court judge Louis Rosenberg, I became a United States citizen. While not a major landmark decision, I was pleased that my stand had remained consistent with my beliefs, and the arguments that underpinned the decision seemed to uphold the best principles of the America I believed in.

One minor postscript is worth noting. Some months after my final citizenship hearing, my sister Susan went to the same office to gain citizenship, as she was about to marry an American. The hearing went well. Just before it was adjourned, one of the immigration officers asked her how her brother was doing. Ha, he remembered! She was pleased to report that I was enjoying my status as a United States citizen and moving forward with my life.

CHAPTER 10 - 1966-1968

Pakistan

My First "Real" Career Position

Iarrived in Pakistan in mid-October 1966 with rather unclear expectations of my role. I knew I was coming to one of the world's poorest and economically least developed nations, one that had exploded into existence less than twenty years earlier in the cataclysm that accompanied India's independence from colonial rule. I knew it was Muslim, but though I'd known Islamic fellow students as friends, what did that really mean? What about my own living conditions? I realized I would have a quite respectable salary, compared with my years as an impoverished student, but beyond that, how would I cope with life in such a different setting? I had no idea, but others had done so, so why not I? I'd been advised I'd need to hire a cook. The idea of servants was off-putting given

Tim trying to fit in while visiting a local health center in West Pakistan

my egalitarian leanings, yet I also knew that I'm no cook and could never handle the local market scene with unfamiliar foods, strange languages and alphabets, and cultural pitfalls galore. The Ford Foundation recommended an experienced cook, and Syed Ahmed Ali turned out to be my resourceful "Jeeves," handling not only the food purchases and cooking, but also managing my large apartment (part of a compound of four units), which meant he negotiated my share of the salaries of part-time staff which included a gardener, *mali*; a guard/watchman, *chowkidar*; and a laundryman, *dhobi*. Mr. Ali, with the formal title of "cook bearer," kept everything in order whenever, as was frequently the case, I was traveling in other parts of the country.

Mr. Ali and the Taj Mahal birthday cake he created for me.

And what exactly did my job entail? Again, unclear expectations as I did not have a job description beyond assisting the Ford Foundation as a junior advisor. The foundation was focused on efforts to help the Pakistan government get a measure of control over the extremely high fertility rates threatening to undermine progress in other areas in which the foundation also had an interest, including agriculture, education, general health, and economic development. In addition to its headquarters in Karachi, the foundation had satellite offices (and guest quarters) in other

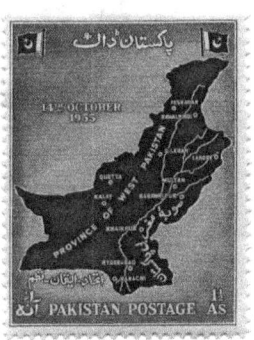

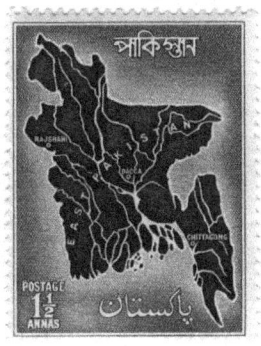

West Pakistan   *East Pakistan*

major Pakistani cities and funded family planning research projects in Lahore and Rawalpindi, as well as Karachi, in West Pakistan, and also in Dhaka, in what at that time was still East Pakistan (later, Bangladesh). I would spend time with the local staff of all these projects, helping them as best I could and monitoring their activities for the Ford Foundation.

Initially, I did this work in close conjunction with my boss, Dr. Sachs, but later he tended to rely on me while he spent more time at headquarters in Karachi working with central government officials.[1] As a liaison between the Ford Foundation and the two United States university–based projects

in East and West Pakistan, along with the Karachi-based Population Council (also partially funded by the Ford Foundation), I eventually found myself involved more directly in some of the research projects of all three of these Ford– Foundation supported projects, but especially in efforts to begin tracking trends in fertility patterns among reproductive age women.

A visit to a district family planning field office in West Pakistan with district family planning and provincial director, W. A. Kahn, right

All these duties allowed me to gain useful experience working with United States-based and local staff in addressing various aspects of large-scale programs to influence people's fertility behavior and practices. I certainly became much more attuned to studies designed to assess and then improve clients' knowledge of family planning methods and then measuring the effects of efforts to improve actual fertility behavior. This research helped the national program identify some of the barriers to changing fertility norms in a highly pronatalist traditional society.

---

[1]One of these officers, Dr. Nafis Sadik, whose office was very near our own Karachi office and with whom we spent much time discussing Pakistan's population issues, later went on to become the head of the United Nations Fund for Population Activities (UNFPA), in which capacity she was the highest-ranking woman in the UN system.

A year later, when Dr. Sachs left to take up a United States position, I was asked by the foundation to remain for a second year and to take on additional duties and was given a pay raise and a title change from training associate to program associate.

From the outset, my duties also allowed me considerable scope to travel into quite remote areas, and thus, to experience aspects of Pakistani life not readily seen by most advisors, and by even fewer tourists. Since most project counterparts were Pakistani,  I was afforded unusual levels of access as I traveled with them whether to monitor surveys or to visit clinics and health facilities.

From the start, I also took lessons in the main language, Urdu, from a local teacher and attained a rudimentary capacity to read the Arabic script, but since English was the lingua franca of this former British colony, there was thankfully no need to try to master all the major local languages.

I also took advantage of my geographic location to fit in personal travel in Afghanistan, Nepal, Sri Lanka, and India, and into rather remote Himalayan mountain sites in extreme northern Pakistan, including Gilgit and Hunza. These experiences fed my wonderment at the variety of cultures and people, and no less the remarkable geographic variability of this ancient part of the world.

India

Sri Lanka

Mt. Everest

Another aspect of my position, for which I remained grateful in my later professional life, was that I became something of a "gofer" for the many international visitors who came either to see the Pakistan program or to assist us in conducting specialized training or undertaking special studies. These visitors were not only Westerners, but I also met and sometimes accompanied officials and researchers from such countries as Egypt, Indonesia, and Malaysia. Not all these experts were in my own field, as I worked closely with other advisors, and even occasionally was able to offer my slide-rule abetted skills in data analysis to our agricultural experts. I still recall well a few days spent sharing the Ford Foundation staff flat in Lahore with a visiting overseas agricultural expert. Over dinner we discussed how neither agricultural development nor population control alone could succeed without the success of the other. He understood the big picture. His name was Norman Borlaug and he would later win the Nobel Peace Prize as the "father of the green revolution." Years later, when he was in his late eighties, I met him again in Atlanta at the Carter Center, where he maintained a close working relationship with former President Jimmy Carter. I was delighted to find that he still saw the big picture.

Our main Ford Foundation–funded population projects were linked to institutions and university population centers in the United States. Through this connection I came to work with and know some of their senior staff, and through them, something of their academic programs, which greatly contributed to my decision to return to the states for doctoral studies in 1968.

Dr. Wishik had left Pitt by late 1967 for Columbia University, and his departure made Pitt less attractive to me. Of the doctoral programs I then considered, the University of Michigan, through the School of Public Health, became most attractive to me. I'd met Dr. Leslie Corsa, who directed the university's Department of Population Planning, in connection with his own earlier work in Pakistan. The Michigan program offered both a strong socio-demographic academic orientation and a more practical and programmatic focus,

which fit well with my interest in program evaluation. An added bonus was that my sister Susan and her husband, Ron Suleski, whom I'd last seen in Taiwan on a stopover on my flight to Karachi two years earlier, had settled in Ann Arbor for Ron's PhD studies. They very considerately offered to start looking for a little apartment for me prior to my arrival.

CHAPTER 11 - 1968-1983

University of Michigan Years

Graduate studies – 1968-1973
  Malaysia, 1970-1971
  DrPH, 1973
Research and Teaching faculty – 1973-1983
  Bangladesh, 1978-1979

A New Life, with Carol

Newlyweds!

It felt good to be a graduate student again, starting in September 1968, and to be able to immerse myself in the intellectual give-and-take of academia. My social life was also not entirely neglected, and within a few weeks I'd met Carol, a graduate student in Asian studies who had previously been a Fulbright student in Pakistan, though I'd not met her at that time. In December of the following year, 1969, we were married in Ann Arbor.

Tim and Carol, newlyweds

Carol by Huron River in Dexter, MI

A few weeks before our wedding, at Thanksgiving, we drove from Ann Arbor through a major snowstorm so Carol could introduce me to her parents near Wilmington, Delaware. I think Carol's parents, Edward (Ed) and Cecile Wrobbel, were a little wary at first about this obviously "liberal" foreign man to whom their daughter was engaged. Fortunately, they welcomed me warmly and the weekend was a success.

Though Carol by then knew two of my sisters and my brother, she had not at the time of our wedding met my parents and the rest of my siblings. We remedied the situation by honeymooning that Christmas with them in England.

Our first home together was a small apartment overlooking the lovely Huron River and the woods beyond it in the little town of Dexter, about eight miles west of Ann Arbor. The daily commute, usually by a scenic back road, was quite pleasant except in inclement weather. Nonetheless, we soon decided to look for a more permanent home in Ann Arbor, closer to our workplaces.

Though in my own coursework I emphasized program evaluation, with additional concentrations in statistics and demographic studies, I was also able (actually, required!) to broaden my studies in preparation for my doctoral prelims, which I completed on the first Earth Day, April 22, 1970. I considered this a good omen, particularly since the concerns motivating the environmental movement had long been close to my heart.

At that time, we were still living in Dexter, where another couple associated with our Department of Population Planning also lived. The night of April 22, to celebrate the successful completion of my prelims, these friends, Dick and Carolyn Monteith, introduced us to the Brandy Alexander cocktail at their Dexter apartment. A heady way to close out our celebration of the completion of my final oral exam, plus Earth Day!

In addition to coursework, I'd been serving part-time as a teaching assistant as one of the conditions of my fellowship and had also begun planning my doctoral dissertation. In May 1970, I left for an initial two-month trip to Malaysia, which seemed a fruitful site for exploring the question of the relative contributions of socio-economic developmental vs. organized program factors in the success of national family planning efforts. The trip went well, and upon my return, I revised and submitted my dissertation proposal to the faculty. With a few modifications, it was  accepted. Basic funding was secured, and I became the first recipient of a new Population Fellows program launched by USAID's Office of Population. With the blessing of the relevant Malaysian authorities, I then headed out again in October 1970 for my field research in Malaysia. Carol joined me a few weeks later.

My fieldwork involved data collection in all eleven states and almost all the seventy districts of Peninsular Malaysia. It was accomplished both by combing through existing data sources and documents at the national headquarters and through surveys I designed and conducted among large numbers of staff. I also informally enlisted the assistance of several United

States Peace Corps volunteers already stationed in different parts of the country, who were happy to be involved and sometimes offered useful insights. Soon after my arrival, I bought a well-used little VW Beetle into which I had to install seat belts before taking on some of the terrain and hazardous driving conditions. Montmorency, as I'd named the car, was our main means of transport, as Carol sometimes accompanied me on these field trips to clinics and government offices.

In exchange for access to records of the eleven state family planning associations (FPAs), and for the government's newer and somewhat larger National Family Planning Board program (NFPB), I happily assisted both these major service organizations in their own research and evaluation efforts.[1]

Carol also did some volunteer work for the FPA and helped me analyze some of the data for the Malaysian Planned Parenthood Federation. An interesting and enjoyable relationship developed with my Malaysian counterparts. Though I was technically still "just a student" (i.e., I had no official government title), I was sometimes asked to be the unofficial stand-in supervisor for the national program's headquarters evaluation staff, and "Dr. Tim" was regularly invited to various planning meetings. Additionally, and partly by request by both the NFPB and the Malaysian Ford Foundation advisor, I was asked to prepare the first draft for the population section of the Malaysian government's second five-year plan. Much of my draft ended up verbatim in that government planning document, though, of course, unattributed. Still, I considered it quite an honor for "just a student"!

Carol took full advantage of our time in Malaysia, sightseeing, taking Bahasa Malay lessons, and learning about Malaysian culture and cuisine from Malaysian friends. While we were there, one of Carol's senior University of Michigan professors, Dr. Richard L. Park, with his wife, Donna, visited us in Kuala Lumpur after an official stop in Singapore. Professor Park was a very dignified and physically imposing man who barely managed to squeeze into our VW Beetle's front passenger seat. Despite this, we had a most enjoyable visit with them. During that visit, he suggested that when we returned to Ann Arbor, Carol might want to consider working for the Association for Asian Studies (AAS), an

---

[1] CYP continued to be an important tool in my work in Malaysia, requiring further adaptation and development. For more detail, see the appendix E.

international scholarly organization, headquartered in Ann Arbor and operating under the aegis of the American Council of Learned Societies (ACLS). Professor Park was the AAS secretary-treasurer, and felt her skills well matched the AAS's needs. Indeed, that's what happened, and Carol spent nearly fifteen years with the AAS.

Malaysia was a lovely experience for both of us in almost all respects despite some underlying tensions related to ethnic, religious, and cultural diversity, which affected relations between the majority indigenous Malays and the substantial "overseas" Chinese and ethnic Indian minority populations, whose arrival from their countries of origin was much more recent. We had good friends in all these groups.

With my data in hand, we returned to Michigan and our Ann Arbor home in the "Old West Side" in August 1971. I spent the next eighteen months analyzing and writing up my research, while again doing some limited teaching and non-dissertation research, publishing a few papers, and undertaking a consultancy for the World Bank (WB) in Singapore in early 1972 as the demographic team member with two WB staffers from Washington.

EVALUATION OF FAMILY PLANNING PROGRAMS:
PRESENTATION OF A GENERAL MODEL, AND ITS APPLICATION TO
THE NATIONAL FAMILY PLANNING PROGRAM OF MALAYSIA

by

John Timothy Johnson

A dissertation submitted in partial fulfillment
of the requirements for the degree of
Doctor of Public Health
in The University of Michigan
1973

Doctoral Committee:

Professor Leslie Corsa, Chairman
Assistant Professor John W. McGuire
Professor Gayl D. Ness
Associate Professor J. Y. Peng
Professor Irwin M. Rosenstock
Professor J. Y. Takeshita

Dissertation title and front piece

Back in Ann Arbor, I sometimes found myself diverted briefly to tasks unrelated to my main professional interest. Perhaps the most memorable and interesting for me, though only a very brief interlude, was a last-minute invitation to join a political science research team from Michigan's Center for Political Studies in the Institute for Social Research (ISR). This team was led by the future United States ambassador to the United Nations, Jeane Kirkpatrick, and involved the delegate study undertaken at the 1972 Democratic National Party Convention in Miami Beach. Some state delegations (notably California) were contested, and these problems necessitated some last-minute implementation changes, thus my opportunity to participate in the quintessentially American political circus of a national convention. It was the year George McGovern won the nomination, but a deeply divided party lost the election to Richard Nixon. I was not a delegate but enjoyed my moments as a fly on the wall and still savor the memories.

Dr. J. Timothy Johnson

Back in my own academic sphere, I successfully defended my dissertation, "Evaluation of Family Planning Programs: Presentation of a General Model, and Its Application to the National Family Planning Program of Malaysia," in early 1973. I was then offered, and accepted in May 1973, what was in essence a postdoctoral research position as the newly minted *Dr. Johnson*. In the next year or two, my role morphed further into a faculty position as a lecturer-instructor then full-time assistant professor position in the School of Public Health's Department of Population Planning.

Over the next years, along with teaching and research, I did occasional consulting work, mostly in countries in which I'd had at least a bit of prior exposure, including Pakistan and Malaysia, and also Singapore, Bangladesh, Nepal, and South Korea. I also took on my share of administrative duties, notably as director of our department's three master's degree programs (mostly MPHs) and served on several doctoral prelim exam and dissertation committees.

Meanwhile, Carol became well established as the office manager and annual meeting coordinator of the Association for Asian Studies headquartered at the University of Michigan, reporting directly to the secretary-treasurer of the organization. She also was asked to represent the AAS on occasion at the coordinating meetings of the American Council of Learned Societies (ACLS), an umbrella group of academic humanities disciplines. Both positions included travel to the large AAS national meetings (New York; Chicago; San Francisco; Washington, DC) and for smaller ACLS meetings in places like Quebec City, San Antonio, and Bermuda, events I attended with her.

This comfortable situation began to deteriorate for me in the late 1970s, as federal government and foundation funding for population programs was reduced, and the state of Michigan imposed further budget cuts. My population planning department was abolished, though not the associated Center for Population Planning, through which I could remain on "soft" money from research and other grants rather than the general department budget. At this time, I began to look toward a future beyond my university and increased my consulting work. Thus far most of my work had been in Asia with at least some direct involvement in a dozen south and southeast Asian countries. In 1978, I added a sub-Saharan African country (Kenya) to this list. Little did I expect that Africa would within a few more years become the main focus of my subsequent overseas work.

But first, back to Asia. I had spent August 1978 in Bangladesh as a consultant to the Government of Bangladesh (GoB). On my return to Ann Arbor, I arranged a leave of absence from Michigan to accept a full calendar year position as advisor to the Family Planning Evaluation unit of the GoB for 1979. My position was funded by the World Bank and the Canadian government's aid agency (CIDA) through the GoB.

I arrived in Bangladesh's capital, Dhaka, mid-January 1979. Only a couple of weeks into this assignment, on February 4, 1979, I got an unexpected midnight call from my sister Joy in England. She was with my mother, and tearfully they told me that my dad had just died from a sudden heart attack. I was shocked, not least because I'd just seen him at Heathrow Airport in London a couple of weeks earlier as I transited from my United States flight to my onward flight to Asia and he'd seemed reasonably fit, though I was well aware of his two previous heart attacks, including one just a year earlier. With the help of Bangladeshi colleagues, I was able to book an urgent compassionate leave flight back to London to attend the funeral and visit with Mother.

A week later, I returned to Dhaka and moved to my now ready apartment. Since it was in a suburb a few miles from my office, I also quickly arranged for a lease of a small car for my daily commute. While it lacked such amenities as air-conditioning, it served me quite well until the end of my assignment in late December.

Being the only westerner in a large office of Bangladeshi staff was an interesting, sometimes difficult, but mostly rewarding experience, especially as the government was seriously ramping up its efforts to bring its high fertility rates under control and our research and evaluation efforts were helping to document what was working and why. In addition to my official duties, I also gave two sets of lectures at the Dhaka University, through which I tried to relate population dynamics with other dimensions of  social and economic development, especially in Bangladesh, and the challenges of measuring the effects of such interventions. These lectures were well attended and well received, though the last of the second series had to be canceled due to a hartal, or student strike, which happened on occasion, causing disruption. This major strike occurred in the wake of the taking of American embassy staff and others as hostages by the Khomeini government in Iran in early November 1979. The situation convulsed much of the Islamic world, including Bangladesh. The United States embassy encouraged Americans to evacuate during the crisis, but since I was scheduled to leave in late December, I chose to continue as best I could with my work whilst keeping my head down as much as possible!

My office happened to be in a building adjacent to an Islamic training school, where I developed a nodding acquaintance with a couple of the bearded scholars. I was quite touched when one of them came over and spoke with the Bangladeshi director. He wished to offer reassurances that, whatever their public demonstrations against the United States might indicate, I was completely safe. In fact, though always wary of misunderstandings, at no time did I feel personally threatened, and indeed my Bangladeshi colleagues and friends were in all cases very personally supportive. Nonetheless, I did feel a certain level of relief when, as originally scheduled, my plane took off for my return to the United States in late December via a stop in London.

I met up with Carol at the home of my sister Elizabeth and her husband, Richard Simon, where we were again able to meet Mother for a visit. They had also arranged for us to attend the Christmas Eve midnight service at Westminster Abbey, a service I found both physically quite chilly and yet spiritually quite heartwarming.

During my year in Bangladesh, I experienced all seasons and types of weather, including notably the heavy monsoon rains that each summer brought life-sustaining and sometimes destructive floods across much of this delta region. These rains can be very disruptive to local travel, and a problem for people like my cook, Lawrence, who would normally visit his village and his family on weekends. He'd take a short train trip to the nearby town of Tongi, followed by public transport to his village. This could be a problem when flood interruptions intervened. Local river transport sometimes got around this difficulty and a variant of that mode resulted in a memorable, and rather unexpected, perspective for me on adapting to circumstances.

I'd enjoyed canoeing in the United States and Canada in earlier years and actually had a bright yellow fiberglass canoe for some years in Ann Arbor, which I would occasionally take out on the Huron River and on small Michigan lakes. In Bangladesh, I became friends with a USAID hydrologist, Dan Jenkins, who had acquired a slightly larger aluminum canoe, and was happy to have me join him to paddle for a few hours on the local waterways. As the waters rose and covered the rice paddies, most of the region became navigable, and as we discovered, we could simply glide over the inundated fields that surrounded the villages, which were on slightly higher ground.

So, could one perhaps canoe cross-country to Lawrence's village? Lawrence liked the idea (maybe he suggested it?) and helped plan this little venture. The weather looked good as we launched the canoe from the Dhaka suburb of Gulshan into a tributary of the main river, which we soon entered, leaving Dhaka behind and heading northward. With Lawrence as our navigator (we only knew the general direction of our destination), the three of us took off just after dawn on a summer weekend. Lawrence had already alerted his home folks of this plan and promised us a good Bangladeshi lunch on arrival. Indeed, the company and repast were both excellent, as Dan and I received VIP treatment.

Too soon, though, Dan and I had to set off for our return, this time without our navigator. Fortunately, the weather held up well for us, and my fears of a monsoonal interruption went unrealized. In the distance, we could soon see the tall buildings of Dhaka. As the sun set, and darkness enveloped us, we found ourselves quite weary from the long day of hot and humid paddling. No GPS in those days, but even if we'd had such an aid, I'm not sure it would have helped with the monsoon-altered waterways. We had considerable difficulty finding our way back to our starting point, navigating in part by following the stars, yet never felt in any danger and eventually did make it safely. Yet, what wonderful memories of that day still linger! Once back, refreshing ourselves with our evening curry meal and rehydrating with both water and beer, Dan and I both knew we would long savor this most enjoyable of monsoon experiences.

That year was not, I'm happy to report, my last visit to Bangladesh, to which I returned with some frequency over the next quarter century. I was witness to some quite remarkable improvements in many national socioeconomic indicators, including lowered fertility and mortality rates, along with much increased prevalence of family planning methods as well as women's education.

Back at the University of Michigan at the start of 1980, I continued mainly as a research scientist, with limited teaching duties. My principal research project, headed by a former member of my dissertation committee, Professor Gayl Ness, involved over twenty Asian countries. A big advantage for us in obtaining the country-level data we sought for our research was the welcome assistance from former graduate students we'd trained from most of those countries. They helped us make further contacts in their countries and facilitated our efforts to gather information during our own field visits to most of these countries. I had previously worked in a number of these South and Southeast Asia countries, and this project brought me back for data gathering in several of these, as well as a few I had not previously worked in. This research was funded by USAID and resulted in several analyses that we presented to them in Washington and in other forums.

During this period, I also worked with some political science colleagues at Michigan on research on the interface of political and population issues, which later was published in a couple of research papers, as well as a brief book, *Births, Deaths, and Taxes: the Political and Demographic Transitions*, published in 1984 by the University of Chicago Press and coauthored by A. F. K. Organski, Jacek Kugler, J. Timothy Johnson, and Youssef Cohen.

On arrival at Michigan in 1968 for my doctoral studies, I had no clear idea what my future career beyond the doctorate might look like. I'd learnt not to make fixed plans, but rather to follow my still-developing life directions. Obviously, though, these directions had gradually become much more focused during the previous years, so I expected that would continue with population and health studies dominating. Those further studies would likely guide my actual path. I thought it most likely I'd then find an interesting position with one of the international groups I was already familiar with, and probably such positions would be internationally oriented, and likely based outside the United States. I had not anticipated that for much of the next decade I would continue to be based at the University of Michigan, as actually happened, and would be a member of the teaching and research faculty there.

I was grateful for the circumstance that allowed both my wife, Carol, and me to engage in work in our areas of professional interest in the richly intellectual and cultural environment of Ann Arbor. In my case, I'd never planned on teaching graduate students, which I found I generally enjoyed. How had this transpired? I was never entirely sure, but I know I was forever after very grateful to find this academic niche in a field I found important to our planet's future, and for the colleagues and students with whom I shared these general values. I would sometimes allow myself to reflect on the strange path that now found me so far from my high school dropout period in a rural North Dakota religious commune!

But inevitably things change, and it was time to move into the next phase of my life and career, as is described in the next chapter, where we find "Atlanta Calls!"

CHAPTER 12 - 1983-2013

Centers for Disease Control (CDC)

Atlanta Calls!

Brown Thrasher &

I began 1982 in a holding pattern professionally. I was open to moving on from academia and began to explore possibilities. Among these, I'd always admired the Centers for Disease Control and Prevention (CDC) headquartered in Atlanta with its global reproductive health focus, so I applied for a promising position as a sociologist/ demographer in the Family Planning Evaluation Program of the Division of Reproductive Health. It had a strong international, developing countries orientation as well as a focus on some of my key professional interests in reproductive health, program development, and program evaluation. I soon learned that I'd been selected! However, due to Reagan-era budget cutbacks and hiring freezes, I did not actually take that position and relocate to Atlanta until September 1983.

At first, Carol was unconvinced I'd want to remain "down South" and it took well over a year of a commuting relationship between Ann Arbor and Atlanta before she joined me permanently in mid-1985. She'd secured an interesting position to replace her Association for Asian Studies (AAS) job at Michigan. Through that AAS position she had come to know Professor Kent Richards at the Iliff School of Theology in Denver, Colorado. Coincidentally, around the time Carol was moving to Atlanta, the Society of Biblical Literature (SBL) was planning a move to Atlanta, where it would be affiliated with Emory University. I don't recall the details, but since my new employer, CDC, was located adjacent to Emory and our new condominium home was also close to both places, Carol asked Professor Richards, who was involved with SBL, about this move in the context of her own search for a position in Atlanta. He replied enthusiastically, believing Carol's past experiences could be helpful in starting up the Atlanta SBL office. Carol's enthusiasm grew when Professor Richards gave us the address where SBL was to be located. It was on our own street, Houston Mill Road! Only a few trees and a parking lot separated our new condo from the new SBL site. We could easily observe the new building's construction from our home. Could this be interpreted, an amused Professor Richards wondered, as a sign of the reality of divine providence? Well, I'll avoid theological speculations, but it certainly was at least a happy coincidence, especially as Carol got the job.

She remained with SBL until 1987, when she joined the then-new Carter Presidential Center and eventually served for more than twenty years in the key role of assistant to the center's president and CEO, Dr. John Hardman, helping to support our former President Jimmy Carter's and First Lady Rosalyn Carter's programs in health, conflict resolution, and general global development.

Carol recognized for her work at the Carter Center by Dr. John Hardman, President Jimmy Carter, and First Lady Rosalyn Carter, October 2003

On a Professional Note

Though CDC hired me principally for my prior and fairly extensive Asian family planning experience, I quickly found myself immersed much more in reproductive health and family planning work in numerous African countries. Indeed, I made well over twenty trips to various African countries before I next returned to Asia. Though African challenges were often substantially different from my Asian experiences, there were also many commonalities. I brought these into play in helping to organize services in African settings, in training staff, particularly in design and management of contraceptive commodity distribution systems, and in evaluating program strengths and weaknesses. By then, there had been widespread adoption of the CYP Index as another practical measure of program performance, and we continued to develop this further.[1]

Family Planning clinic Bangladesh

Our CDC work was largely funded by the United States Agency for International Development (USAID), with which we often worked closely in the field and sometimes at their Washington, DC, headquarters. My activities required working with national decision-makers in the involved countries and with private sector and multinational donor agencies, including the UNFPA, and the World Health Organization (WHO).

While the work could be frustrating, it was also always challenging and rewarding. There was powerful compensation in the satisfaction of seeing improvements in services, and in seeing women come in to obtain care and contraceptive supplies from functioning systems run by staff who understood the importance of their work. Along the way, I was also continuously learning from the those with whom I worked and to whom we provided training as they labored at the interface between the governmental and private sector infrastructures

Family Planning clinic in Nigeria

[1]Additional information can be found in the appendix E.

and the populations in need of such attention. My admiration for the dedicated work of these women (and some men) under extremely difficult circumstances remains enormous: they are a noteworthy contrast to the image of inefficiency, corruption, and hopelessness which was the other side of the picture in much of Africa. Working with them also encouraged me to return, time and time again, to settings that otherwise

 would hold little attraction for me. What else, would induce me to visit Nigeria a total of twenty-five times, and visit almost every state in that large and unruly country?

Family Planning clinic in Sierra Leone

From 1983 until my retirement, I typically traveled on overseas assignments four to six times each year from the CDC headquarters in Atlanta. Our work was principally funded through USAID's Office of Population, with which we worked closely. Fairly soon, I became the deputy to our project director at that time, Dr. Leo Morris.

In 1991, the USAID and CDC's Division of Reproductive Health (DRH) switched from an annual planning and funding arrangement to a five-year planning cycle, and I was asked to take the role of project director, providing general oversight of all our varied USAID-funded activities.

Our main activities, besides the logistics systems and contraceptive management work I've already mentioned, were in conducting national reproductive health surveys in many countries (though mostly in Latin America, with our Spanish- and Portuguese-speaking staff), in epidemiological training and research, and later in refugee and conflict-affected populations. In all these areas, I was supported by excellent colleagues, both at CDC and in USAID's Washington offices, to which I was a frequent visitor for the next fifteen years. Throughout these five-year periods, I also continued as a frequent visitor to many developing countries.

My Washington to Atlanta travels as a civil servant weren't without some intriguing moments. This one was particularly notable: I was not the only passenger waiting in standby mode for a flight from Washington, DC, to Atlanta in early 1995, hoping to get one of the few remaining seats. Already in line ahead of me was the tall and unmistakable civil rights and political leader, the Reverend Jesse Jackson. I discreetly pointed him out to a CDC colleague, who already had secured a seat assignment. She alerted me that also in the standby group was our local Georgia congressman, Newt Gingrich, who had quite recently become Speaker of the House and was making his influence known. His political views were almost the polar opposite of Jackson's.

Final seat assignments were announced, and both Gingrich and Jackson were called to board. The last standby to board was Johnson, given a boarding pass for aisle seat 38C. As I approached the back of the plane, it dawned on me that this was the last row (a noisy one, next to the rear-mounted engine!) and just ahead of me, Newt Gingrich was easing himself into seat 38A, the window seat. Leg space in economy was not designed for Jesse Jackson's long legs as he maneuvered into the middle seat. More compact in build than Jackson, I could have fitted better into that middle seat, but Newt and Jesse were already in a conversation (that largely continued throughout the flight), and my offer was declined. However, for his comfort, Jesse found it necessary to leave in a raised position the seat divider between his seat and mine, which of course did nothing for my comfort level but also made it difficult not to eavesdrop on their conversation (upon which this discreet civil servant chooses to decline to comment). I did briefly join their conversation and was quite happy to accept their offer to both sign my Delta ticket stub to commemorate this strange meeting. Did this encounter in any way change my basic impressions of either man? Again, discretion prevails!

On a Personal Note

In September 1991, my mother passed away at the Darvell Bruderhof community in Sussex. She had been in declining health for some time, though not critically ill, so I planned to detour through England to see her during my return from another of my periodic Nigeria visits. Sadly, this was not to be. I got a call that she had passed away while I was at the USAID offices in Lagos. As in 1979 when I'd interrupted my Bangladesh work to return to England for a few days following my dad's death, I arranged for a quick trip back to England to join my United Kingdom family in saying farewell to Mother.

Rosie at Guy and Eleanor's graves in Bulstrode Bruderhof Cemetery, April 2010

This time, arrangements were made jointly by the Bruderhof and our family. There was a Bruderhof "love meal" and service for Mother at Darvell (which I missed, as I had not yet made it back to England), with a follow-on service at the Bulstrode Bruderhof Cemetery a day after my arrival for non-Bruderhof relatives and friends. My mother's younger brother, Tom Dutton, a Methodist minister, presided. This was also a time for us to sing some of the songs of our earlier lives and enjoy meeting and greeting old acquaintances. Simple adjacent plaques for Guy and Eleanor mark their common final resting place.

Lessons from Extensive International Travel

My extensive international travel experience led me to develop habits and approaches to maintaining my physical, emotional, and mental fitness to optimize my own effectiveness both while traveling and when on location. For example, when crossing multiple time zones, as I often did, resetting one's circadian rhythm at the destination was often best accomplished by incorporating regular exercise routines, to the extent possible, into the required changes in working and sleeping hours.

What sort of exercise, for both health and pleasure? My main ones were usually walking and especially jogging. For me, as a practical matter, this was mostly solo, as I often traveled alone. However, what one actually did was often dependent on local practicalities and preferences. In some cases, it was possible to enjoy more social group exercise. I discovered, even before I went to the CDC, an international running group that operated in some countries I visited called the Hash House Harriers (HHH). I ran with HHH twenty-seven times in Bangladesh, and sometimes in other countries in Africa and Asia. Joining this group also brought me into areas and situations I would probably not otherwise have experienced, such as the hill area outside Addis Ababa, Ethiopia, where we once accidentally flushed a hyena out of the bush, and an encounter in Bangladesh with a strangely acting dog, immediately suspected to be rabid, so that prudence suggested we scatter to regroup later. Yet, solo running, unconstrained by others' schedules, was my usual mode, along with a good bit of walking.

Not all countries are equally conducive to running, and I'm well aware that in many cases women simply could not be as free to engage in such exercises as men. In a few countries, however, women were more welcome to join in such exercises, and I've personally enjoyed mixed gender runs in several countries. I usually kept a record of my daily exercises, which was also a helpful reminder of some of the observations I made along the way. Most of my running was done very early in the day, often starting before full daylight, to take advantage of both the cooler hours in often tropical climes and the fact that far fewer people are usually out so early.

The need to maintain adequate hydration, whether with exercise or just in general, is a recurrent theme among travelers. So, it was for me, though local circumstances could prove a bit problematic, particularly during the fasting month of Ramadan in some countries I worked in. Even for this non-

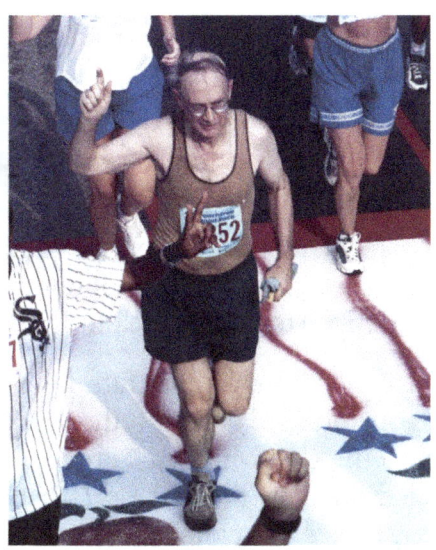

Tim running in the Peachtree Road Race in Atlanta, July 4, 2000

Muslim, it seemed somehow wrong for me to bring liquid sustenance into the office, and I generally adhered to local norms of daytime fasting. I was all the more grateful when on one hot day a refreshing midday cup of tea was brought to my office desk in Bangladesh by the kind tea lady. These jogs, and related experiences, remain among some of my best memories of several countries in which I traveled.

On a very different earlier occasion in Pakistan I accidentally learnt of the nonequivalence of gin and water in terms of urgent rehydration. I'd spent a long, hot, and dusty day in a jeep in the Sind desert and was feeling the effects of dehydration well before I got back to the rural rest house in which I was staying. At this place, I knew bottles of boiled water would be waiting, well cooled, in the common refrigerator. Thirstily, I opened one, and rather than finding a clean glass, took a good swig straight from the bottle. Big mistake! The clear liquid was pure gin, belonging to a fellow infidel, but unmarked. I ingested very little as the burning taste of the gin induced an immediate gag reflex, saving me from further intake. I immediately switched to the water I'd been craving, but had to explain to the owner of the precious gin what had happened. He was an American engineer (from Texas, as I recall), who was assisting with a large natural gas development project. Fortunately, he was very understanding! Besides reinforcing the lesson that gin is no substitute for good, plain water, our subsequent interaction also reinforced that gin and tonic was a far pleasanter beverage for me than straight gin.

Not all health encounters were as benign as my gin incident. Despite one's best efforts, travel may involve difficulties and unexpected situations. I had visited Nigeria many times before this trip in 1994 so I was not particularly concerned on my arrival in Lagos, the nation's commercial capital. However, by experience and reputation, I knew to be careful. After long and tiring flights from the United States via Europe, clearing airport immigration and customs obstacles, a long taxi ride to Lagos's Victoria Island suburb, (the location of the United States embassy and the USAID-preferred hotel), I was looking forward to checking into a hotel that was well known to me, the Eko Meridien. By the time I got there, it was already late evening.

As it happened, two other CDC staffers, Mike Deming and George Stroh, were also staying at the Eko. They were acquaintances, though not in my division of the CDC. Their presence would prove to be very helpful.

After hotel registration, I headed to my assigned room on the fifth floor. There I discovered a couple of problems, including damage to the lock. I left my bags in the room and returned to the check-in area to request a room change. It was promptly arranged for a different floor. I then returned to my original room to transfer my bags. I was carrying my trusty and well-worn leather briefcase along with a plastic bottle of drinking water I'd need for the night. There was almost no light in the corridor, and that wing of the hotel seemed rather deserted. In near darkness, I fumbled with my key and the recalcitrant lock. Suddenly, from behind, I felt an arm around my neck. I was very tired and jet-lagged, so it took me a second or two to realize what was happening: I was being mugged! In my briefcase were all my personal documents, and a substantial amount of cash, and I was down a dark hallway alone with my assailant.

As the assailant tightened his grip on my throat, I knew my predicament was dire and that I was quickly losing consciousness. Since he was behind me, I used my elbows to try to pummel him off me, as fight-or- flight reactions pushed me into survival mode. Partly reflexively, and partly because I was off-balance, I dropped to the floor, momentarily also knocking him off balance and off me, allowing me to breathe. As I stumbled up to face him, he pulled back a couple of feet. I could now see him, albeit rather indistinctly. Perhaps instinctively I kept him back by defensively waving my briefcase and water bottle at him. At that point, he pulled out a knife. Still using the briefcase and water bottle as shields, I continued to defend myself, but I knew I was at a severe disadvantage.

Remembering a lesson I'd learned from a colleague, I yelled and screamed for help as loudly as I could. I did not know whether anyone could hear me, but realized the assailant also did not know, and would not want to be caught committing this armed robbery. To my relief, down the hall doors opened and two or three men emerged. My assailant ran farther down the hall and onto a stairway. I was safe, though bloodied, as evidenced by both sleeves of my shirt.

Later that evening the assailant was caught and identified by hotel security as a recently dismissed employee who evidently still had easy access to the premises. Now he would face Nigerian justice, whether through the court system or through the summary "justice" that often bypasses it. For the remainder of that night, I was grateful to accept Mike Deming's invitation to move into his room and sleep on his couch.

Next morning, relevant USAID staff and others were fully briefed on the episode, and for quite a while thereafter USAID advised against the use of that hotel for its consultants.

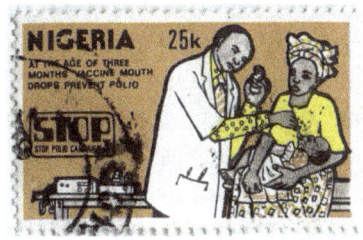

I temporarily moved to the USAID guesthouse. A couple days later, still hoarse and with my throat still raspy and uncomfortable, I was able to start my intended tasks in other Nigerian states. Though my throat was still affected by the throttling, and remained so for some time longer, Nigerian colleagues who traveled with me did most of the talking for the next week or so. When I returned to Lagos, it was to a different hotel!

An Unexpected Professional Opportunity

While Africa and Asia were the primary foci of my work, the fall of the Soviet Union gave me unexpected but fascinating opportunities to consult periodically, beginning in 1994, in Russia and five other newly independent states of the former USSR.

Having grown up in a world largely divided into the Western and Eastern political blocs, I hardly thought it likely I'd ever have much chance to know what lay behind the iron curtain, beside what I'd gleaned already from history and literature. Then, in 1991, the Soviet Union dissolved. Within a few years, I found our CDC reproductive health division, with my own direct involvement, participating in efforts by the United States and others to help improve reproductive health and family planning systems and services in the former USSR. The emphasis of these efforts was to have greater availability of contraceptives and more contraceptive methods, thus lowering their high abortion rates. In the process, I had unusual access to some of that world and was glad to avail myself of undreamed of experiences. They included guided tours, as honored guests, of the Kremlin in Moscow, the Hermitage Museum in St. Petersburg, and the site of the assassination of Tsar Nicholas II and his family in Ekaterinburg when the Russian Revolution had ushered in the era of the USSR.

History, for me, was now made much more real by such visits, such as stopping a couple of miles from the site where the Soviets had brought down the U-2 spy pilot, Francis Gary Powers, which became a major international incident and an embarrassment for the United States in 1960 at the height of the cold war when I was still in

college. Now, two American colleagues and I found ourselves discussing this incident with Russian counterparts and hoping we were collectively helping to usher in a more cooperative era between former adversaries.

The reality of my trips was often less lofty, as evidenced by an episode from an internal flight from Donetsk to Odessa, Ukraine. Two CDC colleagues and I were on our first visit in April 1995 and traveling with more seasoned Ukraine travelers. Prior to this flight, we'd taken an overnight fourteen-hour train trip from Kiev to Donetsk. This flight was our next segment, a couple of days later. Our bags were loaded by airline staff into the front of the plane, separated by netting from the passengers further back in the same main cabin. Arriving in Odessa, and on the airfield a short distance from the terminal, we disembarked. It was then we learned we would have to retrieve our own bags from the plane. Apparently, this was the standard practice, not something simply reserved for the foreign visitors!

In the five years following my first visits to the former USSR, I experienced some positive developments regarding increased reproductive choice and improved client/provider relationships in three "stans" (Kazakhstan, Uzbekistan, and Kyrgyzstan). During two visits to Russia, three to Ukraine, and a very brief detour to Moldova during my first Ukraine visit, I was afforded a chance to enrich my own understandings of these countries, contribute in small ways to improved international  relations and, more particularly, to developments in managing aspects of reproductive health improvements. Along with our contraceptive logistics work, we were involved in launching the first reproductive health surveys in those countries. In part through these activities, we helped local healthcare professionals in their own efforts to shift their countries' overwhelming reliance on induced abortion to gradual but substantially increased use of modern contraceptives and to improved capability for women to make their own contraceptive choices.

Winding Down My Professional Career

By the end of our third round of five-year agreements, and after passing my sixty-fifth birthday in 2004, I decided to turn over the responsibility for negotiating the next agreement to younger colleagues. In early 2005 I announced my retirement, to become effective at the end of August, allowing time for an orderly and smooth transition, especially of my management responsibilities.

Yet my retirement was not complete, as I worked out an arrangement with CDC to remain there as a part-time contractor, to continue to assist in international reproductive health activities. The arrangement also allowed me to do some consulting with the National Institutes for Health and a couple of other agencies. But by late 2011, I was glad to be retired from all but some very limited "guest researcher" activities at CDC as I transitioned into full retirement in 2013.

My decision in 1982 to join the CDC had been a good one. The work fulfilled my personal desire to combine academically sound approaches with practical applications to address social issues through population and family planning in a variety of international settings. I admired and gained much from my CDC colleagues and others around the world with whom I worked. And Atlanta turned out to be a fine location for Carol and me, as we remain here to this day!

To Tim Johnson on the Occasion of his Retirement from CDC

Within the walls of CDC,
You'll find him – Johnson, Timothy.
British accent, scholar's mien,
But oh, the places he has been!

His office filled with books and charts,
He takes statistics much to heart.
Thoughtful, logical, precise,
Tim is also very *nice*.

Tim is just the perfect boss –
Always rational, never cross.
His mind retains each small detail.
He reads and answers each e-mail.

You'll find, when you have a chat,
He's not your *usual* bureaucrat.
How many others, would you say,
Grew up in far off Paraguay?
Yet learned no Spanish from the sojourn –
He somehow came out speaking German!
And what spot could be remoter
Than a farm in North Dakota?

Although not giv'n to strong emotion,
To fam'ly planning he's shown devotion.
Who else, you know, would make a career a'
Helping people in Nigeria?

Tim knows logistics to its core.
But wait! He knows a great deal more.
Eclipses, dogs – there is no theme
But which his knowledge runs into reams.

My daughter shuns all other media –
She thinks Tim's her encyclopedia.
Want to know of stars or atoms?
Take those questions and fire 'em at him!

Great to work with, fun to know –
Tim, we're going to miss you so!

Retirement poem by Susanna Binzen, August 2005

EPILOGUE

Reflections on Our Improbable Journeys, from Later in Life

I have been writing about my Bruderhof experience intermittently for much of my adult life, in part instigated by others who were curious about my upbringing, or who shared it, and in part by my own desire to record it, as I did in little diaries during my late teens in our early and turbulent years in the United States.

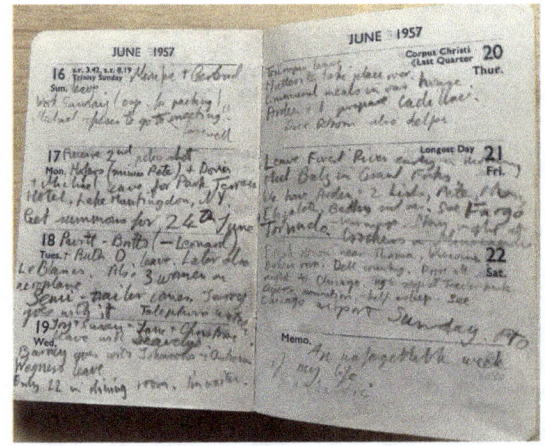

On later rereading, my diary entries sometimes triggered memories of the events that culminated in our family's fragmentation — my expulsion from the commune, the expulsion of two of my siblings and then of my parents, which resulted in their return to England with their four younger children.

Once estranged from the community, and as my own life proceeded in unexpected ways, I found myself looking more broadly at the forces that shape our lives and the lives of those around us. My general interest in history, geography, and social structures, both as academic pursuits and as they related to my own growth after leaving the Bruderhof, also contributed to a desire to tell my parents' story, in part perhaps to understand my own. Certainly, some of my siblings felt similarly, and some urged me to take this project on.

It is my hope I have made clear that some of the appeal of my parents' idealism did transfer to me and my siblings. However, the interruption of our parents' journey affected us all. Through their engagement and disengagement with the Bruderhof, we learnt useful life lessons, applied as we each moved on with our own versions of meaningful lives.

Considering My Parents' Improbable Journey

As I shared in chapter one, the real start of Guy and Eleanor's journey was during a difficult time in Europe and the world, and more specifically for them in England in the later 1930s, and in the aftermath of the First World War with its effects largely expressed by the economic depression. It was also the time of the rise of Nazism and other expressions of reactionary nationalism with ever increasing threats of international conflict. These currents engendered countervailing political and religious forces in several European countries, notably both Germany and Britain, with their calls for nonmilitary solutions. Though ultimately these movements failed to halt the march toward the war that was to engulf Europe before 1940, it was the setting for the commencement of my parents' own journey as they joined with the non-nationalist, socioreligiously based Bruderhof. Both the religious message of this group, and its expression through trying to live by their conception of the early Christian churches, remained central to my parents' beliefs from those earliest years.

Though they remained true to the essentials of their original vision, that vision also changed as their world changed, reflecting developments in the broader society in which the commune was embedded, changes

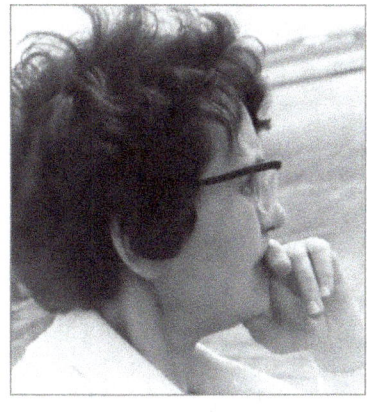

Eleanor and Guy

in their own geographical locations (England, Paraguay, and the United States), and in the growth of their family to eight children. They could not have anticipated these changes, and in fact, they were unable to reconcile their original vision within the substantially altered Bruderhof of their later years.

I believe, however, that both their response to these challenges, and the influence they had on their children, can in some ways be seen as an extension and adaptation of their original vision, for which there of course never was a clear blueprint beyond selected New Testament passages, amongst which the Sermon on the Mount was most cited by them.

Did they see their expulsion from the commune as a failure for them? I do know it was a severe test of at least some of their commitment to, and faith in, "brotherhood." Had they broken the religious and social contract of their lifelong vows, or was the Bruderhof no longer the same entity to which they had committed themselves?

Within a few short years of my own and two siblings' departures, followed closely by my parents' expulsion, the entire community was convulsed by an existential crisis. About half of both the South American and European groups found themselves suddenly expelled and excluded from the communal religious society they had built. Primavera and the existing English and German communes were abandoned as the much more recent United States communes were established and became dominant. Different interpretations of this crisis and its outcomes are obvious in some of the writings after that time from those who remained compared with those who left, as well as by some more neutral observers. Relatively small differences were magnified by some individuals with their own agendas and viewpoints, and by religious certitudes which worked against diplomacy and compromise in adapting to the emergence of inevitable tensions from communes expanding into new geographic regions with different sociocultural and economic realities.

To those who left, voluntarily or not, did the schism represent a failure of the dream? Though many experienced great difficulties in finding a new footing, especially when it involved starting anew in great poverty and often with young dependent children, most did eventually develop new meaning in their lives. My parents fell into that group. I don't think they regretted their part in an experiment in communal living which had, after all, shown promise of achieving some of the things they valued. Had they not shown that people of different nationalities could live together harmoniously and constructively, with a common set of beliefs and purpose guiding them? Nonviolence had not failed them in establishing bonds with others. Had they not shown, by example, that at least in some circumstances and durations, barriers of class and prior socioeconomic background could be largely overcome in working for the common good? So maybe this was at least a qualified success, from which other societies could perhaps learn, while also recognizing the pitfalls which led to the end of this particular venture, at least for them.

After their return to England in 1961, my parents' overriding concern became one of survival and reestablishment for themselves and the children who had not yet struck out on their own. Yet even here, though new realities could not be ignored, they never abandoned their earlier vision, and continued to try to instill in their children some of the values that still guided them.

They'd given much to their dream of communal living, and never completely abandoned it in their own minds. This was often a theme in their get-togethers with others who left ("Leavers") from the time of

The Johnson family at Eastbourne with Grannie and Grandpa Johnson, October 1961

the major upheaval in the entire Bruderhof organization in the 1960s. Though they clearly felt that the Bruderhof had, during that period, lost much of what had guided it in earlier years, they also felt a strong loyalty to the ideals which had sustained them, and other idealistic members, through this journey.

What are the criteria by which to measure the success of a utopia? If one lacks a clear blueprint, agreement cannot be reached, since one is left with post hoc observation and subjective judgment. To my parents, the general blueprint was defined by certain key biblical interpretations, particularly of such New Testament passages as the Sermon on the Mount and the Acts of the Apostles, with their interpretation of the latter leading to their belief that communal living was the closest fit for them. I don't think either of my parents ever adopted a literal dogmatic interpretation of the Bible, as some other members seemed to, especially with the more evangelical outlook of some of the later United States joiners. Certainly, their children all had to conform in general terms to Bruderhof behavioral norms, yet both with their own children and others who questioned stated beliefs, my parents were not threatened by honest questioning. They were also never "anti-science." When I, as a youngster, told my father of my questions about "the life" and my future in it, he made clear that guidance during his youth came more from his own sense of "right" and his conscience than from formal religious rules. "Let your conscience be your guide" struck me as being as sound as any dogmatic formula, and not too different from the "Veritas et Virtu" motto of my later undergraduate university.

Considering the Gradual Discovery of My Improbable Journey

My own intellectual and practical divergence from "Bruderhof life" could not be described as planned. Rather, it was the convergence of influences, stemming from the gradual realization that the Bruderhof path could not be mine, and a consequent searching for meaning in my life, independent of how I'd been raised. Over time, while I'd accepted many of the values exemplified by Bruderhof teachings, I also recognized that there might be other less restrictive ways that might be more compatible with my own developing sense of my place in the human family than I'd find in a group requiring me to essentially give up thinking for myself. So, to "voluntary servitude" and submission to some sort of arbitrary decision-making process in the guise of received religious truth, no thank you!

The process was gradual in early years, especially in England, but could perhaps have been predicted in broad outline already before our family emigrated to the United States, and the personal disruptions this entailed for my teenage self. My two years in North Dakota, including my forced "dropping out" of the local public high school to work on the farm at Forest River, followed by my brief final year of high school in Pennsylvania and my expulsion by the community at that time, forced on me decisions I would have preferred to make more gradually. Necessity, for better or worse, became the accelerator of changes that were already underway in my personal evolution. But toward what?

The language of religion, including its expression in the Anabaptist Bruderhof, did not hold answers for me, though from the community life and many fascinating individuals who had thrown in their lot with it I did learn valuable lessons, albeit not unique to that tradition. Respect for life, for hard work, and especially for the notion that people could live and work in harmony, were all values inculcated by the Bruderhof, and values I chose to hold on to, even when I saw less admirable traits sometimes displayed.

I found more meaning and personal affinity in the exploration and examination of ideas. For example, though our formal education at Wheathill had shortcomings, in other respects it was exceptionally rich. Its history and internationalism at that time exposed us to other influences. International visitors were frequent, and I recall early exposure to the still relatively new United Nations (UN), including more than one visit by a UN official, from whom we learned more about this interesting sounding organization and its  various international health and conflict resolution aims. For me, it added to my interest in geography and other topics from my own personal exposure, supplemented by stamp collecting, reading, and especially our visitors. I was not the only one who welcomed the perspectives brought to us by international youth campers, by anti-apartheid South Africans, vegetarians, Esperantists, etc., and my personal exposure benefited from Dad's guest warden duties. A well-rounded education? Perhaps not a typical English education, but overall things at Wheathill seemed to be moving in what I considered a positive trajectory.

The Bruderhof in Wheathill, though choosing as a matter of religious principle not to become directly involved in national partisan politics, could fairly be described as generally left leaning. Many members had early links to the British Labour movement, with its pacifist and egalitarian principles, which they felt were also consistent with their own religious and communal underpinnings. In this, they partially overlapped with social, educational, and even political reformers and philosophers of late eighteenth to early twentieth century Europe and America. Even as youngsters, we had some exposure to some of these ideas, and their supporters as well as opponents.

At the University of Pittsburgh, I determined quickly that the natural sciences would be my focus, and in my second year settled on bacteriology as my major with chemistry as another area of interest, along with minor emphases in geography and English. Among other things that fascinated me in microbiology and bacteriology was seeing in rapid sequence what could happen in closed systems, as represented by microorganisms in a nutrient broth, when they quickly outgrew their resources and sought to adapt to the new little toxic ecosystems they were creating. Were we seeing, in microcosm and greatly accelerated time frames, the fates other species have endured over the eons, and were there lessons in this for our own species? If so, could conscious interventions serve to change trends for humans, or were we too destined soon to be the destroyers of our environment? Such thoughts, combined with memories of Malthus and my own observations of high fertility populations, human and otherwise, competing with other claimants to those limited resources all fed into questions not only of "Why are we here?" but also, "Since we are here, can we make 'here' a better place?" Musing further, was I in the process of developing my own guiding philosophy, akin to a "religious calling," so perhaps not so different from what had motivated my parents and others a generation or two earlier?

One difference was that my parents saw subservience to a religiously based church community as a requirement for achieving fulfilment and voluntarily decided on this path for themselves. For me, distressing though it was, expulsion from the community was the launching pad for viewing new possibilities, which emerged over time.

Now, I could begin to explore those questions of life's meaning and purpose in the framework of what I might contribute to whatever I discovered in that journey. My coursework was a good start, as I sought both to indulge my innate curiosity and to fill in gaps I was already aware of in my earlier education. From the start, I gravitated toward the natural sciences, and particularly the biological sciences and chemistry, along with a fair dose of mathematics and physics. This was both because I had some aptitude in these more quantitative realms and because at that point they held more interest for me than such areas as economics, sociology, and psychology, and certainly religion. That was partly because of lack of exposure with and familiarity with these areas, and definitely because the Bruderhof had made me a little gun-shy about what I saw as more subjective and qualitative areas, where I could not use facts and numbers against other's "feelings" about topics. Subjects such as history, geography, and literature seemed to me to fit a different dimension, and I'd study them where I could, but at that time they were secondary to my concentration in the natural sciences.

There was no clear road map that led to my eventual focus on population as a field of study. Professional engagement and opportunism were as much in play as any initial clear cut goal. Yet both my background and my educational choices played into the general direction my life was taking. Peace activism of various sorts ranked high for me, along with a desire to use my developing skills toward effective interventions to shore up values I felt supported human betterment, particularly through education and health. Could health and medicine, either through research or actual person-to-person contact, be ways for me to contribute? In general, my coursework led in that direction and added a possible international component, but as I ventured further into the social sciences, the horizons seemed to widen. Demography — broadly, the study of human populations — entered both my lexicon and my consciousness as an academic area with real-world ramifications. Hmm, were Paraguay, Malthus, Hutterite fertility, and even those test-tube bacterial cultures in the university lab, coming together in some strange alchemy to suggest my future directions? Well, not exactly, but they could not be ignored!

Reflections on My Bruderhof Journey in a Larger Context

For about a quarter century after my departure in 1958, I charted my own way, with very limited direct involvement with either the Bruderhof or those who'd left it after I had, other than my family. What contact I still had tended to be somewhat accidental. Yet, like many Leavers, I did eventually find myself participating in informal networks of other Leavers with an interest in their experiences and the challenges they encountered after leaving. The most significant network was through KIT.

KIT was the acronym for "Keep in Touch" among Bruderhof Leavers who chose to maintain some contact with other Leavers. At its most basic, KIT was whatever its participants considered to fall under the "Keep in Touch" rubric. No formal mission statement or objectives were initially identified, beyond just: "let's keep in touch."

The first KIT newsletter appeared in August 1989, and within a couple of years a ten-page monthly letter was sent to a mailing list of about five hundred addresses.

As in most ventures, one determined and charismatic individual can be identified as both catalyst and leader. In this case, it was Ramón Sender

KIT group reunion, August 1991

Barayon, who self-effacingly described himself as the "accidental" founder of KIT. Ramón, with his first wife, Sibyl, had come to Woodcrest in the late 1950s, with their young daughter, Xaverie Sender. Ramón left in early 1959; Sibyl and "Xavie" remained. Ramón was permitted only sporadic contact with Xavie, and was informed, well after the fact, that she had died of cancer in 1988, at age thirty-two. Thwarted in getting information from the Bruderhof and in visiting his two young grandchildren, Ramón contacted first one, then more, Leavers, in late 1988. This contact network rapidly snowballed, mostly by word of mouth, and by 1989 began to be identified by its participants as KIT.

A recurrent theme was that KIT helped individuals deal with the emotional trauma of being cut off from their families back in the Bruderhof. This allowed them to take such Bruderhof ostracism less personally. KIT enabled people to find themselves as part of a wider family, to some extent substituting for the "Bruderhof family" they had left behind.

That said, a substantial but unknown proportion of Leavers were not involved with KIT. Some appeared to be totally lost to follow-up, even to family members who may not even have known whether they were still alive. Others kept in touch with their own family members outside but did not wish to be involved with other Leavers.

Visual record of unrecorded recorder medley by Joy, Elizabeth, Margaret (Johnson cousin), and Barnabas at the KIT group reunion, August 1991

KIT, with more or less success, provided an opportunity to:

- Meet to reminisce about Bruderhof experiences,
both positive and negative

- Understand one's Bruderhof heritage and hurts stemming from
that heritage

- Build bridges with the Bruderhof for those within and
without who cared to be in contact

My participation in these networks led me also to delve into our common background and into consideration of some of the positive and negative aspects of the Bruderhof experience, particularly for children, and how it varied over time and place. Were there common threads and differences, for example, in child-rearing in such groups as the Israeli Kibbutz movement compared with the Bruderhof and other Anabaptist groups such as the Hutterites, Mennonites, and Amish? I also met numerous times with groups of former members, and with people who had studied the Bruderhof from a more academic perspective. With this personal background and interest, I did indeed feel prepared to try to bring into focus some aspects of the life my parents lived as well as my own.[1]

Though in many ways so different from the world we currently live in, my parents' world was also a dangerous and difficult place in late 1930s Europe where their journey together began in their native England. Like many, they sought a better way and felt they had found it in an already existing international faith-based "community of goods," the Bruderhof in Germany, where it was founded. Most members were German, who by the time my parents joined had emigrated to England after essentially being expelled by the Nazis for their religious and therefore also political communal life. In England, "Bruderhof" was rendered as the "Society of Brothers." My parents' decision to join this group initiated for them a quarter century of life in an evolving community, which tried to maintain its core beliefs and social structures even as it was buffeted by forces beyond the community's control. It also launched the "Johnson Eight," as eventually my parents had eight children, whose arrival would inevitably affect the dynamics of my parents' subsequent path.

---

[1]The above paragraphs are taken in part from the essay, "A Community of Bruderhof Leavers: Reflections on the 'KIT/ Hummer Process' by Timothy Johnson and Ruth Lambach, 2013. It is available online to read and download in its entirety at: https://shorturl.at/ofzmi.

I've tried to tell the story in this memoir as it played out for my parents and their children as they moved between three continents, and as the Bruderhof itself evolved in response to internal and external forces. I have also tried to present not only some of the history of that journey, but also some of the context for what transpired for my parents and their children, and the whole community, as it continued to evolve through periods of crisis and relative calm. I hope this memoir is helpful and interesting not only to people who knew members of our Johnson family, but also to others who found themselves cast aside as the community itself evolved in ways that were not always predictable and that often paralleled parts of our family experience.

Besides "Bruderhof Leavers" (by choice or otherwise), I hope this book is interesting to some members of the current Bruderhofs and more recent Leavers but more broadly, I hope these reflections speak to members and Leavers of other utopian ventures, and maybe add perspectives to their own searches for meaning. And for others, I hope they can just enjoy comparing their own paths with the unanticipated journeys recounted here.

I close with no grand theme or revelation, but rather two thoughts.

First, I am not alone in finding disturbing similarities between the pre-WWII period of western Europe, and notably Nazi Germany's frontal attack on "rule of law", and the situation we now find ourselves in, especially in the United States, where "rule of law" is also under severe attack.

In that earlier era, society as a whole underwent enormous and unpredicted upheavals. I've explored some aspects of one small group that was a bit player in that drama, the Bruderhof. It was buffeted by history's larger currents while trying to navigate its own course and hold on to its own values. My parents and their growing family stayed afloat on that current for more than two decades and on three continents within this group.

Then, they found themselves involuntarily starting anew in the early 1960s in a world greatly changed from the one they'd voluntarily left in the late 1930s as they sought a new societal order.

My second closing thought is actually a question. Beyond "viewing with alarm," what can we do, individually and collectively, to counter what many see as major radical threats to civil society and rule of law? When does our lack of pushback become complicity with what we see as plain wrong, both in our dealings with our fellow world citizens and with a decently sustainable world? It seems that, once again, our consciences are being tested.

We know what happened in that earlier era. But have we, collectively, learnt from those real-life lessons, or are we destined to relive some of them? Future historians will look back both at how the United States as a society, and beyond that the rest of the world, navigated these upheavals, and how different populations within society were impacted and responded. I hope they'll be able to record something more positive than I fear!

In closing, I return to a notion that has been a recurrent theme running through this volume that I think applies to "what now" for each of us in these times: accepting someone else's dogma is likely to be less fulfilling to oneself than adopting the idea of "to thine own self be true" or, more commonly, "freedom of thought." For many earlier Bruderhofers and those who later had to choose other paths as Leavers, the song "Die Gedanken sind Frei,"[2] loosely translated as "My thoughts, they are free," was a useful reminder that how we responded to the world around us to move forward in our own lives and relationships could be our own choice. May it be so!

Tim Johnson

2025

---

[2]The song's history and lyrics in English are widely available on the web. I encourage your investigation.

APPENDICES

APPENDIX A

Were There Lasting and Discernable Influences from the Bruderhof Experience for the "Johnson Eight"?

None of the "Johnson Eight" ever actually joined the Bruderhof, though all were born there between 1939 and 1954 in either England or Paraguay. All remained in the Bruderhof until 1958 when I was expelled. Soon two of my next three siblings were also "sent out." Our departures, and what precipitated each one, were a reflection, in part, of the growing tensions within the Bruderhof that eventually resulted in my parents' ejection (with their younger children) in 1961 from Oaklake, and their return to England. That year, my sister Joy was "sent out" separately from Bulstrode Bruderhof in England.

All six sisters and Eleanor at Cheney Cottage in Shoreham-by-Sea 1964

Rosie, Joy, Elfie, and Rebecca in Cornwall, 1964

Because they were still young when our parents were expelled, my younger siblings had shorter durations of Bruderhof life, but even the youngest, who was aged six when she left, has memories that stay with her from those turbulent early years.

Are there discernable influences from the Bruderhof experience in the Johnson children's lives?

To consider the question, I prepared a simple chart with categories that included educational choices, professional/occupational interests, religion and life philosophies, global/international interests, and family and children orientation. I then measured each sibling on the criteria to see if any common threads might emerge.

Herewith, a few personal observations:

While certainly absorbing the Bruderhof's and our parents' respect for physical, no less than intellectual, pursuits, I think we all strove for levels of more formal education to help us not simply to engage in work that interested us, but that would allow us to examine both our own lives and our societies without restrictions imposed by outside agencies.

Particularly from their own midtwenties until their separation from the Bruderhof, religion was a much more overt aspect of our parents' lives than those of their children. I believe our parents' strong commitment to the Bruderhof community, and its religious underpinnings, served as an inhibition to any tendency by their children to align with, or commit to, any formal "theism." With the exception of Elizabeth, who is very actively involved in her local church, none of us has embraced church culture, although we may well have fond memories of Christian festivals like Christmas and Easter, and their associated carols and hymns, and value the religious works of great composers. For the rest of us, early Bruderhof experiences became a shield against commitment to any "received religion," though not against the searches for wisdom common to major religious and intellectual traditions.

Values absorbed from the Bruderhof, and more directly from our parents, substituted for formal adherence to Bruderhof doctrines, flawed and inconsistent as they had proven to be for us. These values included such basics as the Golden Rule, and its extensions of respect for others and for nature, an emphasis on searching, in one's own way, for "truth," along with a skepticism of anyone claiming to know "truth" or the "true path." I think in our own ways, all of us still valued our parental and early Bruderhof idealism of improving the lives of people, both near and far, but not the trappings of religion or the strictures of Bruderhof "early Christian" interpretations. None of us has put gaining material goods as a first object in life and this, also, I feel is a heritage of the Bruderhof.

Departure from the Bruderhof had not been a choice for any of us. Yet it did open up different sets of opportunities in life trajectories for us all.

From my teenage perspective as an involuntary high school dropout charged with tending to the several thousand chickens in a rural North Dakota commune, and without imminent prospect of improved personal circumstances, I certainly would not have foreseen how things would change for me within just a few years.

Among the eight of us, we'd eventually acquire credentials in fields I had not yet heard of and find satisfying careers in professional fields beyond the agricultural and community manufacturing enterprises we might otherwise have expected in the Bruderhof. For my siblings and me, our futures would include several advanced degrees, civil service and academic careers, and a good bit of international work in occupational fields in numerous countries on four continents.

In all these pursuits, I believe our parents' guiding philosophies remained a major influence.

I hope to clarify the commonalities in a brief summary of the principal activities of each of the Johnson children:

Tim

Since my own trajectory following my 1958 expulsion has already been described at length, let me skip to the next in age, my sister Joy.

Joy

Joy, born in 1941 in the Gran Chaco in Paraguay, was a very able student and would have liked to become a physician. However, the Bruderhof reflected Western gender-based role-model biases of the time and she was pointed toward nursing instead. Though Joy remained at the North American and then English Bruderhofs for a year or two after others of the older siblings had effectively left, she too left the Bruderhof after returning to England. There she trained in London as a nurse and midwife, and remained active in this profession for some years, including after her marriage to Bob MacDonald in August 1967 and the establishment of their own family, two sons and a daughter. Bob, an engineer by training, was business oriented and established a couple of very successful businesses in Surrey that became something of a family enterprise. Joy continued with some nurse-midwifery and added other interests, taking her back to more academic yet also practical concerns, and resulting in her obtaining a master's degree from the University of Surrey in therapeutic counseling and psychotherapy.

Barnabas

Barnabas was born in Loma Hoby, Paraguay, in 1943. In 1958, almost simultaneously with my Bruderhof departure, Barnabas was sent to the Olney Friends Boarding School, a Quaker school in Ohio, where he thrived. After his graduation, he moved to Cleveland, Ohio, for work and further schooling. Barnabas remained in Cleveland after my parents' 1961 departure and return to England.

After getting a degree from Western Reserve (later, Case-Western Reserve) University, he was accepted by Harvard Law School. His legal career, after various positions in the United States, took him and his wife, Lowry Wyman, also a lawyer, into activities involving the former Soviet Union, and initially into the Baltic States, and then Central Asia. (By happenstance, I was able to visit him and Lowry in Kazakhstan in 1994 when one of my CDC assignments overlapped with a much longer tenure there for them). Later, they also spent some years in Armenia, another country struggling at that time with the transition from the USSR to democratic independence and establishing a political framework for "rule of law" primacy in the post-Soviet era.

As Barnabas and Lowry observed the real life impacts of these changes for the people with whom they worked, I believe that for my brother his own commune and cooperative experience must in some ways have come together with the legal-scholar aspect of his training to give him some unique perspectives and insights. How would individuals react and adapt as the structures of the collective collapsed and they rebuilt their lives without the collectives' social support structures they'd relied on? I think it played at least a subliminal role in his and Lowry's "feet on the ground" work in some former Soviet states.

Susan

Susan was born in Paraguay in 1944 and was eleven when we moved to North Dakota. Like Barnabas, she graduated from the Olney Friends Boarding School in Ohio. She returned to England with the family but soon decided to return to the United States, and more specifically to Pittsburgh, where I was living at that time. Her work and college studies there were paused by her marriage to Ron Suleski, a student who had spent some time in Asia and who was planning to return there for further study. Soon (mid-1966), he and Susan departed for Taiwan. Again, serendipity (or kismet?) resulted in my managing to visit them in Taipei for a few days and staying in their little apartment in October of 1966 as I traveled to Pakistan for my own first overseas professional posting. That was my first real taste of Asia. A couple of years later, after they'd returned to the United States for Ron to complete his doctorate from the University of Michigan, they were very helpful in getting me settled into Ann Arbor when I arrived there in 1968 for my own doctoral studies. Susan completed her BA at Michigan. (Later, in 1982, she completed a master's degree at the University of London.)

Elizabeth

Elizabeth, perhaps in part because of her earlier polio and the physical limitations it posed, had always been very studious. She was the last sibling born in Paraguay, in Loma Hoby in 1947. In 1961, Elizabeth was the oldest of the four daughters still at the Oaklake Bruderhof when my parents were expelled. The family settled in Cleveland, Ohio, and, as I understand it from her, Elizabeth was initially hoping they'd soon return to Oaklake as a family. That was not to be, as six months later they returned to England.

There, she thrived in the public school system. She then attended the University of Edinburgh, where she nurtured her love of history and politics. I think it may have been around that time that she became our unofficial family historian. She placed highly in competitive civil service exams and joined the Department of Health and Social Security, which directly and indirectly led her to several interesting positions. Among other things, as a "principal" she served in the House of Commons, providing on-the-spot facilitation to department ministers during parliamentary debates on social security matters. In her biography, Barbara Castle, who was the secretary of state for Social Services (whom I would have enjoyed seeing as the first female prime minister, though that was not to be!) mentions Elizabeth several times. Since Elizabeth's position was a nonpartisan civil servant posting, she had earlier served in the same capacity for Tory secretary of state Sir Keith Joseph.

As a preteen, at the time of the Festival of Britain in 1951, I'd visited London for my first time and been awed by the experience, including a visit to the Houses of Parliament. Now, some decades later, my younger sister worked there. I was impressed! Still a bit later, when Carol and I visited London together, Elizabeth arranged for us to sit in the visitors' gallery of the House of Commons, from which we could observe a parliamentary debate. It was a nice window to a heritage and traditions my earlier life had largely bypassed.

Meanwhile, Elizabeth had met Richard Simon, a young lawyer, and eventually they were married and settled in London, where they raised their three children. I first met Richard with Elizabeth in early 1974 during their engagement. They'd arranged to meet me and one of my Michigan faculty colleagues, Professor Jason Finkle, during our several-hour London (Heathrow) layover as we flew from Michigan to meetings in Islamabad, Pakistan. They kindly took us from the airport to a lovely and historic pub near the airport. Jason was even more impressed than I was to learn that not only was this one of England's oldest such establishments, but that reputedly it was the site where, in 1215, a probably not very happy King John had stayed as he made his way to Runnymede to seal the Magna Carta and mark another inflection point in England's history. Though impressed, the combination of our previous night's long flight from Detroit and the warm meal and warm beer all conspired to relax Jason enough that he soon fell soundly asleep by the warm open fireplace.

Elfriede

Elfriede was born in January 1949 at Wheathill, the first sibling born after my parents returned from Paraguay. She was six when we left for North Dakota, and twelve when she returned with the family to England. Because of the age difference, and my own expulsion while they were still young, and then their departure for England, I did not really know well any of my younger siblings, both during their last three years at Oaklake and especially after their return in 1961 to England. Other than one visit to England for about three weeks in the summer of 1964, I had even less contact from 1961 to 1968, when I returned to the United States from Pakistan with a stopover in England.

I did get to know Elfie a little better when in early 1969 she decided to leave England on a one-year visa to stay in Ann Arbor, Michigan, where Susan and Ron had moved after Taiwan. I'd also recently moved there for my doctoral studies.

Elfie had some affinity for late 1960s American counterculture, and much enjoyed such things as the folk music for which Ann Arbor was known. Along the way, she and a friend also managed to participate in the massively attended Woodstock music festival celebrated in New York's Hudson Valley in August 1969.

Back in England, she obtained a teaching degree from London's Goldsmith College. While hitchhiking and youth hosteling in the United Kingdom, she met David Gloag, a young Canadian. They moved to his home area of British Columbia, where they established their own home. For many years she ran a childcare business from their north Vancouver home. David became a lifelong teacher in the local school system.

I think it fair to say that Elfie was the most "turned off" among my siblings by her Bruderhof experiences, particularly in her last years there, and showed least interest in this part of her past. Indeed, Jane Elfriede, known as Jane in our earlier years, chose to drop that part of her name at the time she left Oaklake. Henceforth, she became Elfie.

Both Elfie and David are nature lovers, and very much outdoor types with strong environmental interests, as they also raised their three sons to be.

Rosie

Christrose, or Rosie, was the second youngest. She was born just after Christmas in 1950 at Wheathill so was aged nearly five when the family moved to the United States, and nearing eleven when her parents and younger siblings returned to England.

I did not see her there until I visited the family in 1964 for a few weeks. It was the "swinging England" of the 1960s. In 1964, both Elfie and Rosie seemed to me to have adapted well to post-Bruderhof life in England, in this era of the mods and rockers, and of course the Beatles, and they were happy to help educate their elder brother about a world they felt he might be missing out on! (He, in turn, was happy to see how well they seemed to have adjusted to their post-Bruderhof life, and how liberating they found it).

Rosie, in particular, seemed to me to have become a fairly typical teenager of that period. Though a good student, in her teen years she was perhaps more interested in enjoying life than preparing for its next stages after completion of her precollege public schooling. Free-spirited and gregarious, she started on further studies at what would later become Brighton University and began to show promise of entrepreneurial talent and future managerial skills.

She married at twenty to Ian Sumner, had Daniel and settled in Wales. They separated, Benjamin was born, and Rosie became a single mother to and principal provider for her sons. She held various positions, including some with international aspects, and senior management responsibilities with The Thomas Coram Foundation for Children and the Fine Art Trade Guild. Through all these positions, she was helped by being very bright and sociable, in addition to her management and leadership skills.

Rebecca

Rebecca, the youngest, was born in 1954, at Wheathill. She was a year old when we left for the United States, and not yet seven when our parents and the four youngest girls left the Bruderhof and returned to England.

After public school, Rebecca obtained her first degree from Bristol University. From as early as I can remember, Rebecca showed an interest in social and political causes and well-informed activism.

In the late 1970s she traveled overland across Africa, and for some months was off the grid so only learnt of Dad's February 1979 death sometime after the event. She then returned to England but soon resumed her world travels.

Her first stop was in Asia, where she stayed with me in Bangladesh for about three weeks before continuing her trip, via several other countries, to Japan. There she remained for close to two years, during which she became much involved with Hiroshima-related antinuclear weaponry and related peace activities.

Peace-related activities encompasses a wide field. Rebecca has managed, in her long activist career, to be involved in many component movements, often in leadership positions. Along the way, she was affiliated with the Greenham Common women's peace activists and with the Campaign for Nuclear Disarmament (CND) and did a stint as regional director with Greenpeace. Her later work led to her obtaining a PhD from the London School of Economics. Though the main focus of her work related to peace and nuclear disarmament interests, she was often able to insert a feminist perspective on this and other global survival issues. (Indeed, I found it difficult sometimes to keep up with the broad range of her work!)

Along the way, Rebecca founded and led the Acronym Institute for Disarmament Diplomacy in 1995, whose name reflects the many groups (and their acronyms!) which shared overlapping interests, particularly in activities related to disarmament, peace, women, and civil society activism. In this capacity, Rebecca gained considerable recognition and support for her peace-related work. In 2017, when the United Nations adopted the Treaty on the Prohibition of Nuclear Weapons, Rebecca saw this, and her role in working toward this outcome, as a capstone to her own efforts.

Along the way, Rebecca cofounded ICAN, itself an acronym for the International Campaign to Abolish Nuclear Weapons. She was still on its steering committee in October 2017 when ICAN was awarded the Nobel Peace Prize! I remember well the morning when Carol and I heard this news on the radio from our local Atlanta NPR station. As it happened, I was to fly to United Kingdom that evening, which allowed me within a few days to celebrate with her and several members of the family.

I'm sure I was not the only sibling who reflected on our parents' earlier and rather different efforts toward world peace and reconciliation and how they might have reacted to Rebecca's Nobel honor. While her approach was different from our parents' eight decades earlier, they would have celebrated her contribution to that part of their own vision. They also would have recognized the searching done by each child for their own life path and celebrated the gamut of contributions to the world made by each one.

Johnson Eight in Rosie's Garden

APPENDIX B

War Orphans

The Bruderhof was well aware, both in Paraguay and England, of the havoc wrought by WWII in Europe and the massive reconstruction and reconciliation efforts. They wished to do their part, consistent with their overall mission, to alleviate some of the suffering. For the Primavera communities in Paraguay this was through helping more than one hundred people, mainly from Germany and the Baltic region, to resettle in Paraguay. From Wheathill, arrangements were initiated for the resettlement of several young children whose parental identity in that postwar period was unknown, and for some about whom little else was known. This turned out to be a long process, but in October 1949, Wheathill welcomed ten "war orphans," five boys and five girls. I'm no longer sure, but believe they were all aged between about six and eleven. Most of these had siblings in the group. Three of the boys were brothers: Klaus, Dieter, and Juergen Holz. Another lad, Herbert Brose, came with his younger sister, Edeltraut. There were also two sets of sisters, Waltraut and Margarethe Meyer, and Ursula and Erika Stosse. Heiner Kopschall came without any siblings, and we knew the least about him. Indeed, at that time neither his exact surname nor date of birth were known with confidence. The ten were housed at Cleeton Court, which had been acquired by the Bruderhof as its third farm a few years earlier and which was located within a mile of the well-established main Wheathill community of Lower and Upper Bromdon.

As planned, at Cleeton Court, Alice and Owen Humphries became the foster parents for this group of German-speaking youngsters, albeit with major support from the whole membership. The orphans were rapidly integrated into the Bruderhof's children's community of somewhat bilingual children, who were encouraged to get to know them, and soon did.

Part of the Bruderhof acculturation was that these children were also "semi-adopted" (my term) into existing families for such events as community

Alice Humphries teaching the war orphans c. 1950

celebrations, birthdays, and holidays, along with "family suppers." Family suppers were something of a Bruderhof institution, providing breaks from the routine communal midday dinner and evening supper routines and allowing for more time together as family units. Single people were invited to these events by families, as further socializing opportunities, as sometimes were children from other families. The "orphans" were also incorporated in these arrangements. Somehow, and happily, Heiner Kopschall became a fixture at our family table and remained so for the next years. He obviously

Heiner (right) with the Johnson siblings (left to right): Joy, Rosie, Barnabas, Tim, Elfie, Elizabeth, and Susan

enjoyed his interactions with both my parents and the older children (me included) who were close to him in age, and with the younger ones, to whom he was soon another "big brother."

This ended when we left England in 1955. Not long after, we learned that additional information on Heiner's background had emerged, which allowed not only corrections on the spelling of his surname and his precise date of birth but also helped him establish some contact with his original family.

Within a few years, most of the orphans returned to Germany as relatives there were located or else drifted away from the community (though often maintaining at least some contact with Alice and Owen). Heiner was the only one of the ten who later returned with his own family (wife Judith had also been a "Wheathill kid") to the Darvel community, where Alice, now a widow, lived.

Decades later in 2011, on a United Kingdom visit for our nephew Daniel Sumner's wedding, my wife, Carol and I made a detour past Darvel. With sister Rosie driving, we decided to swing through Darvel for old times' sake. At the entrance, talking with a neighbor, whom should we see in the vegetable garden

Heiner with Rosie and Tim, March 2011

but our old friend Heiner, whom I'd last seen in 1991 at my mother's funeral! Rosie stopped her car and called to him. "Rose!?" he said, as he walked to the car.

She replied something like "And here's someone else you know!"

"Timmy!" he exclaimed, as the years rolled back. There was mutual delight in seeing each other, as he told us about his large flock of children, and by then, grandchildren. We managed a photograph of our reunion, which sadly was our last, as he died a few years later.

APPENDIX C

Palmgrove: Observations from 1994

Nigerian reflections - "The Bruderhof's Palmgrove Community:
A Visitor's Report" by Tim Johnson and published in the KIT
Newsletter, April 1994

Note: This essay started as a brief letter to KIT (Keep in Touch) [1] since several people had asked me about my February visit to the Palmgrove community in Nigeria. As I wrote, I felt I should make my comments available also to people I know at the Bruderhof who otherwise might not see them in the KIT newsletter. It might be unrealistic to hope that my observations and reflections could contribute to intra-community debate and discussion of this venture, yet I felt that I should disseminate them, in the spirit of hope for more open and better communication between KIT folks and the Bruderhof. I sent it to a few Bruderhof members as a concrete effort to provide some external feedback.

During a February 1994 visit to Nigeria (my nineteenth in the past eleven years) I found myself unexpectedly visiting the state of Akwa Ibom in Southeastern Nigeria to review certain aspects of that state's family planning program. People from at least two hofs had previously suggested that if I ever found myself in the vicinity of Palmgrove I should try to stop in, but since my recent work has been more in the mainly Muslim north of Nigeria, I'd indicated that such a visit was unlikely. Yet, there I was, not only in Akwa Ibom state, but in the small town of Abak, headquarters of the local government area (LGA), in a rural area where Africa's first Hutterian colony is located.

As my colleagues and I finished our work at the main LGA public health center in Abak, I discreetly inquired whether anyone knew the location of this group. Yes, indeed! Moreover, if I'd like, the nurse in charge of the clinic would be glad to help me locate this place she'd

[1] Keep in Touch (KIT) is an organization of Leavers from the Bruderhof. More information can be found at perefound.com /kis.html.

heard about. So, off we went, first to a rural clinic near Palmgrove, and then to Palmgrove itself, with an entourage besides our driver of four Nigerian colleagues.

Obviously, having several others with no Bruderhof background is not the best way to ask the particular questions one might have. Yet it was interesting to hear the questions my Nigerian teammates, all well-educated and with a strong background in social and health concerns (two nurses, a physician, and a social scientist) asked about this unusual venture, before, during and after our visit. Fortunately, all were intrigued as to what I was taking them to and eager to accompany me.

(Later, as we drove away, I had, of course, to go into long explanations of what my connections with this group were as we reviewed our impressions of what we had seen and heard.)

From a hard dirt road, some distance from the main highway, I saw a large building under construction and guessed this might be part of Palmgrove. This surmise was confirmed by the appearance of a bearded westerner, who turned out to be the genuine Manitoba article, I believe named Zach Waldner. He directed me a short distance further to the main hof area.

This main compound of perhaps twenty-five acres fronts on the public road and has been enclosed by a high fence with a gate to the road. I gave the gatekeeper my name, and somewhat allayed his suspicions by naming the two people who I thought might be there, even though one (Don Alexander) had left some time earlier. The other was Burgel Johnson, née Zumpe, married to Martin Johnson. While it turned out that she and several others were unfortunately gone for the day, my credentials were sufficiently established that I was taken to meet a Hutterian-garbed lady I had noticed across the courtyard. She turned out to be Martha Wiser, married to Steve Wiser, and remembered by me as Doug and Ruby Moody's little daughter.

Martha invited my colleagues and me into the Wiser living room, where she and her daughters took on the role of gracious hostesses, plying us with peanuts and liquid refreshment, very welcome at mid-afternoon in that climate!

The nurse, who has overall responsibility for the 170 public sector family planning clinics in this state, not only felt a professional bond with Martha (also a nurse), but also indicated to me later that she hoped to visit again, having been quite fascinated and impressed by what she observed yet having many questions.

One question she did not ask had to do with the community's position regarding family planning, so clearly an issue with great health and economic implications to such underdeveloped countries as Nigeria. I think that for the two nurses, it was just a reasonable assumption that any other nurse would support child-spacing activities, even if not fertility limitation per se, as a matter of routine. What is the present Hutterian Brethren (HB) position on reproductive choice by couples? My colleagues didn't ask, and neither did I, so I don't know whether they have rethought their traditionally anti–family planning position in the changed cultural and health context of rural Nigeria.

After refreshments, Danny Meier, who I'd last seen in Primavera in the 1940s, gave us a quite comprehensive tour of the premises, and explained the various construction, agricultural, health and other projects underway while introducing me to some of the folks we encountered, both Nigerian and foreign.

Though short, our visit was both interesting and enjoyable, and all of us were grateful to the folks who, on such short notice, made their unexpected visitors welcome.

A ninety-minute visit, even supplemented by substantial previous reading and thinking about this venture and substantial exposure to various aspects of Nigerian (and other African) culture, was too brief to answer definitively most of the questions that have concerned me since I first heard of this experiment, yet not too brief to give some impressions.

The geographic and physical aspects were more attractive than I'd expected, with slightly rolling terrain and rather pleasant vistas. Considerable thought had obviously gone into the layout of the buildings in this little community, so that it had a quite homey "Hutterisch" aspect to it, with living quarters and community departments surrounding a central courtyard area. The dining/meeting area, still under construction, is somewhat off to the side, at the opposite end from where the chickens are penned. Potable water is provided by a deep borehole tube well. The notoriously unreliable national electrical system is supplemented by the community's own generator.

Close behind the buildings are the garden areas, with the staple cassava dominating, but also with a variety of other fruits and vegetables, including pineapple and papaya. To me, this was somewhat reminiscent of Loma Hoby and Ibate, circa 1947, though Palmgrove's acreage was substantially smaller.

The community makes much of this experiment as a model for third-world development, and initial appearances of ongoing construction, simple yet very livable quarters, and efforts toward self-sufficiency do seem impressive. The notion of complete participation by all in the community's development, while not as unique as the community seems to believe (witness, for instance, the Peace Corps approach, and numerous smaller and lesser-known projects around the world) certainly has much to commend it.

Unfortunately, to serve as a model for emulation elsewhere, several problems need first to be resolved, of which the first is the sheer problem of the intensity of monetary and material inputs this effort requires. It was admitted to me that virtually all the efforts to date are financed fully from abroad, with very substantial sums of money, and that this will have to continue for the foreseeable future. At this point, though steps toward self-sufficiency in agriculture, and longer-range financial viability through such activities as palm-oil processing are underway, there is no evidence that this can become a truly viable and sustainable venture, let alone a prototype for third-world development, since the unique conditions at Palmgrove simply cannot be replicated on a massive "institution-building" scale.

Among these conditions are very substantial infusions of technical and monetary assistance, which on a per capita basis are far beyond levels any developmental agency has at its disposal at a national level in any country. Second, while the number of skilled outsiders willing to work in this one small village will assuredly have some short-term local value, how likely is it that such an infusion of effort can be diffused to surrounding areas? I expect there will be some spillover effects, but without the corresponding monetary support level, and the pioneering spirit of this Hardi band, I think the project is destined to achieve far less than it hopes.

Ultimately more disturbing to me, is the sense that in its cheerfully optimistic reports on Palmgrove in such publications as *The Plough*, the HB blithely ignores or denies very deep-rooted cultural and social differences on which this well-intentioned effort is likely to founder, though when and if that happens, it is apt to be attributed to human failure to follow the will of God, or some such tendentious reasoning. Among major differences, let me note just three which, interacting with each other and in combination with the issues noted in the preceding paragraph, may prove insurmountable.

First is education. The formal level of education appears far lower among the Nigerians, on average, than among their westernized coreligionists, and is also substantively different in ways which do not make for a comfortable base of common experience for future resolution of inevitable misunderstandings.

The second concerns differences in working habits, or degree of conformance to the Weberian Protestant ethic. The pattern of early afternoon activity I observed at Palmgrove showed a distinct divergence between the Western and Indigenous participants, in levels of postprandial physical exertion. How can these differences be reconciled? Indeed, should they be? If so, my personal bias would suggest that the more relaxed local pattern, developed over generations of exposure to the enervating local climate, and perhaps culturally and physiologically more appropriate, should be allowed to dominate. (Do I hear some distant echoes, something about "mad dogs and Englishmen," venturing in the noonday sun?)

Third, and ultimately perhaps the most difficult in this socio-cultural triad, are the differences between the two groups which I believe will surely arise on issues of sex and marriage, and more generally on male/female roles. In my years of periodic exposure to Nigeria (and other African societies), I have found the attitude to human sexuality to be generally much more relaxed and matter-of-fact than not only the ultra-Victorian virtual denial of sex typifying the Bruderhof, but even of most contemporary Western society. One does not need to make any value judgments on these divergent perspectives of sexuality to recognize that they are apt to lead to profound disagreements when at some future date circumstances force them to be faced, as will assuredly happen.

These are all aspects of cultural differences which ultimately cannot be glossed over by pretending either that they do not exist, or that expressions of shared belief in a set of Hutterian principles can somehow overcome them.

While I believe that the differences alluded to are essentially cultural, rather than racial, one must recognize that there are potentially profound ramifications which are both cultural and racial, if not for the community as a whole, then at least for individuals who, given the community's "constrained choice" pattern of couple formation (and dissolution) may find themselves at some point trapped in situations with which their own cultural background leaves them ill-prepared to deal. For instance, I understand that Nigerian law in most instances gives precedence to the husband/father over the wife/mother with regard to children. Apart from the potential separation of couples for church-related reasons, the political volatility of that part of Africa suggests that this too could raise painful situations. I also foresee the day when a young mixed-race communitarian finds him/herself expelled into a world in which the inevitable problems of survival may be further compounded by questions of racial and cultural identity. To what extent has the community addressed these issues? Very little, I expect.

To conclude this already overlong commentary, let me note that while my comments suggest both skepticism and concern about the Palmgrove venture, I should also make clear that I sensed that the HB participants are intrinsically well-motivated, decent people who believe in both what they are doing and how they are going about it. They are working hard, in accordance with their own perceptions of what is involved in achieving "brotherhood," to live up to their beliefs. I also believe, however, that their sense of the divinely guided rightness of their vision has left them tunnel-visioned in a number of ways that will ultimately work against the success of this effort, as most of them currently envision it. It will certainly never fit the social patterns of the eastern United States communes, as I'm sure the HB increasingly recognizes. Just possibly, I dare however hope, Palmgrove might evolve and blossom into an indigenous blending of some of the nobler values of the Hutterian community with more traditional and culturally appropriate social structures. At the very least, its evolution should provide a rich lode of information for students of the human condition.

APPENDIX D

Additional reading regarding the Bruderhof:

- **Allain, Roger.** *The Community that Failed: An Account of Twenty-Two Years in Bruderhof Communes in Europe and South America.* Carrier Pigeon Press, 1992.

- **Bohlken-Zumpe, Elizabeth.** *Torches Extinguished: Memories of a Communal Bruderhof Childhood in Paraguay, Europe and the USA.* Carrier Pigeon Press, 1993.

- **Britts, Philip.** *Water at the Roots: Poems and Insights of a Visionary Farmer.* Plough Publishing House, 2018.

- **Manley, Belinda.** *Through Streets Broad and Narrow: A Woman's Ongoing Search to Find a Christian Pacifist Lifestyle, Including a 17-Year Sojourn in the Bruderhof Communities.* Carrier Pigeon Press, 1996.

- **Mow, Merrill.** *Torches Rekindled: The Bruderhof's Struggle for Renewal.* Plough Publishing House, 1989.

- **Rubin, Julius.** *The Other Side of Joy: Religious Melancholy Among the Bruderhof.* Oxford University Press, 2000.

- **Zablocki, Benjamin.** *The Joyful Community: An Account of the Bruderhof: A Communal Movement Now in Its Third Generation.* University of Chicago Press, 1980.

APPENDIX E

Note: The CYP Index is referred to periodically throughout Part Two of *A Path Too Narrow?* Including this appendix is, I admit, a personal indulgence as it allows me to reflect on a theme that coursed through my professional decades. Interested readers will find in it further background on the development and application of this measure of contraceptive protection and overall family planning program effectiveness, and why its creation was important. The piece may also make clearer some of what motivated my own professional path.

Thoughts on the Development of a Key Output Indicator for Family Planning Program Evaluation – The CYP Index

By the time I completed my master's degree in 1966 at Pittsburgh's Graduate School of Public Health, I had a pretty solid grounding in population studies, including the available analyses of the relationship of population and some associated indicators such as education, health, and economic well-being, both in the United States and globally. I had also been introduced to various public health program interventions, including family planning, and the value of data and its management in developing and then guiding efforts to improve programs. I was becoming increasingly aware of the politics of many programs, and the different interests at work both in defining program goals and in allocating limited resources (mostly money and staff).

While maternal and child health (MCH) was a well-established segment of public health, population, as an area with major overlap with MCH but also with other realms of health, was relatively new. To some, it remained rather controversial. By the early 1960s this attitude was changing, particularly with the development of new and more effective contraceptives, notably oral contraceptive pills and intrauterine devices (IUDs). Concurrently, with already substantially lowered infant mortality rates and continued high fertility rates, population growth worldwide was beginning to raise alarms about the range of likely impacts of unchecked population growth on other aspects of socioeconomic development. Academics, especially in the United States and Europe, were increasingly turning attention to such questions. Organized nongovernment programs, notably including various Planned Parenthood affiliated groups, were established in several countries. In the 1950s a few government programs, though mostly quite limited, were also being established.

Among the early government programs were those in India — a pioneer in promoting large-scale IUD and male and female sterilization programs. Some of India's very varied states experienced rapid and notable early successes, though also controversy in their implementation. Overall, there was an increasing acceptance in the 1960s and beyond of the idea that high fertility rates were ultimately incompatible with other developmental goals, such as agriculture and education. In general, this was true particularly for much of Asia, followed by Latin American and Caribbean nations, with most of sub-Saharan Africa progressing much more slowly at that time. The 1960s were also when my own interest in population was beginning to come into clearer focus.

Also at this time, demographers, economists, and scholars in various other disciplines noted increasing divergence in population growth rates between more and less socioeconomically advanced parts of the world and speculated about the causes and longer-term implications of such disparities. In academic circles, the term "demographic transition," was popularized as a descriptive shorthand summarizing the different patterns observed over time in more developed western economies, including the United States and most of Europe, compared particularly with less economically developed southern regions in much of Asia, Africa, and Latin America.

My own interests too were moving into international socioeconomic development, and I was beginning to look for opportunities in this field.

Pakistan, India's geographic neighbor, also was among the regional pioneers in recognizing, from a general developmental perspective, that it needed to increase its people's knowledge of family planning and access to family planning methods and services if it was to bring its high population growth rate down to levels more in line with the already substantially reduced mortality level. Pakistan's success in the first half of the 1960s was very limited, in part because the program relied mainly on the existing inadequate health infrastructure. However, some local officials, aided by external consultants, helped identify some of the weaknesses, and this led to some quite radical upgrading of family planning efforts being introduced for the second half of that decade. Key to this was the elevation of family planning activity within the central and provincial governments. This secretariat was headed by a rather charismatic senior civil servant, Enver Adil, who had the full backing of the country's president at the time (Ayub Khan) and had a substantial and much increased budget available to him. In addition to local resources, some foreign advisors and consultants to the government were also recruited to assist in various capacities. This soon included staff from the United States-based Ford Foundation and Population Council, along with the Swedish International Development Cooperation Agency (SIDA), and soon thereafter, the United Nations. Though initially the United States government was not a participant, changes in the United States soon resulted in USAID representation and assistance.

It was around this time, while I was still a student in Pittsburgh, that I first became aware of the Pakistan program. This was mainly through the return to the University of Pittsburgh of Dr. Samuel Wishik, from his role in Pakistan as an advisor aiding the government in revamping its family planning program. After his return to Pittsburgh, where he was professor and associate dean in the Graduate School of Public Health, he continued an advisory professional relationship with the Pakistan program. At the same time, he and I got to know each other, and soon thereafter he became my academic advisor for the remainder of my Master of Science program, after he became aware of my interests. He was investigating the establishment of an academic population track at Pittsburgh and was exploring his ideas of what this might include. Along the way, and less by design than necessity in the absence of such a track, I had unofficially created a program for myself which included coursework outside the School of Public Health to meet my own developing interests in population's role in development, and in the relationship of family planning (FP) programs to overall development and particularly to maternal and child health improvements. This allowed me both to be something of a sounding board for Sam Wishik's own ideas of what such a track might entail, and to become involved in his continuing Pakistan work. It was through this, and in following up with some of his ideas for measuring the progress of FP programs in Pakistan, that in 1966 I first became exposed to his idea of using an index for contraceptive coverage that could be a useful "outcome" measure for program administrators. This was the CYP Index, which was an abbreviation for "couple years of protection." The basic idea was that programs needed some sort of aggregate measure of protection against unwanted or mistimed pregnancies provided by all contraceptive methods available through the program. Besides CYP, various other terms were considered in early years, including "women years" and "women months" of pregnancy protection, but over time "couple years" became the most widely used term. Thanks mainly to Dr. Wishik's work, Pakistan's program was the first to rely heavily on this output measure.

Acceptance of this indicator was by no means immediate, nor universal, as legitimate concerns about it had to be addressed from the start. Over the next years, I frequently found myself engaged in those discussions and efforts both to refine the initial crude indicator and to promote its use, along with other measures of program performance. Overall, it has weathered well the test of time, as it became widely used in large scale programs over the next decade. It also became the backdrop for some of my activities through those later years, both in my teaching and research, and then in a major component of my work at CDC in helping USAID in assessing program coverage and in forecasting contraceptive needs.

Let me elaborate!

In October 1966 I arrived in Pakistan for my first post-master's international assignment in the population/health field through the Ford Foundation and its Pakistan office in Karachi. I had no prior relevant field experience, but Pakistan proved to be an excellent site for rectifying this with its recently reinvigorated national program along with considerable support, both financial and technical, from external sources including some by the Ford Foundation. National goals for fertility reduction over the next five years were established, in terms of crude birth-rate reductions, along with a budget to support national activities to greatly increase the people's awareness and knowledge of family planning and the adoption of smaller desired family size norms that would be needed to achieve such reductions. National systems needed measures, as the programs expanded, to quantify "non-births" and assess achievement of these national goals. How do you measure how many condoms are needed to be as effective as an IUD?

Monthly reports were generated, both for outputs and for levels of staff by different categories of workers. These certainly served some of the needs of top-level administrators in allocating resources, but they were recognized also as being very limited beyond generating crude trend lines. A key question was what effect these efforts were having in terms of fertility reduction, for which better indicators would be needed. In the absence of direct fertility measures, could the application of the CYP Index serve as such an indicator? Critics correctly pointed out problems with estimated prevalence of contraception being used as a proxy for births delayed or prevented. Indeed, ideally, one might prefer more direct measures of fertility levels and changes, yet these would require intensive and expensive surveys of fertility and prevalence of contraception, which realistically could only be done at infrequent intervals. Also, while this approach might be considered for national overviews, it would not be very helpful to program managers who wished to track performance patterns among different subpopulations, and relate these outputs to the resources, especially of staff, required to achieve them.

Might there be a more easily determined proxy measure of performance, based on such service statistics as "program users," which could inform and guide managers? This was the genesis of CYP as a program performance indicator based on the contraceptive coverage provided by different methods given by organized FP services. Most academic treatments of the advantages and deficiencies CYP were at that time in working papers and limited circulation manuscripts. The first more generally available discussions of this indicator appeared in a specially commissioned 1968 edition of the well-regarded journal *Demography* to which the Pakistan government's secretary and commissioner of FP had been invited to submit an article. He asked for assistance in preparing this, which Sam Wishik and I provided, as footnoted in the article.

This paper appeared under the name of the FP commissioner, Enver Adil, as a brief article titled "Measurement of Family Planning Progress in Pakistan." This contained a discussion of the CYP Index and its application as a management tool in the Pakistan program. Since the index was new, the estimated levels of coverage for each of the methods were rather crude and were little more than educated guesses. The same issue also carried a somewhat critical review of CYP, and its conceptual deficiencies, but did not provide alternate measures to help guide managers at more local program levels. Such critiques, along with lessons learnt through experience and research in later years, led over time to more refined versions of the CYP Index. Meanwhile, the late 1960s marked the start of CYP as the dominant program output indicator for family planning programs which, albeit with changes, has been used by major programs and donor agencies in subsequent decades.

My own involvement with CYP continued directly and indirectly throughout the rest of my professional life. On my 1968 return to the United States from Pakistan, I resumed doctoral studies, with an emphasis on health and family planning programs and their evaluation. By then I was at Michigan, but I still maintained close contact with Sam Wishik, now at Columbia University, where he and his staff continued to explore ways to assess program outcomes, including through more refined CYP measures. This brought me to Columbia several times, especially in 1969, though I was mainly in Michigan, busy with coursework and with developing ideas for my doctoral dissertation. The latter eventually took me to field research in Malaysia, where Carol and I spent a good bit of 1970 and 1971.

In the dissertation itself, I was interested in variations in the level of success of the national family planning across the eleven states and more particularly the seventy administrative districts of Peninsular Malaysia, and in distinguishing how much these differences were due to measurable program factors that could be directly influenced by policymakers and managers, compared to less direct program environment factors, such as urbanization, education and ethnicity. CYP came into this picture as one of the measurable outputs related to district level contraceptive use levels. This required me to work further on adapting this index to the emphases of the Malaysian program, which was unusual in its heavy reliance at that time on contraceptive pills and the service networks through which these were made available. In discussing my research methodology, I also discussed the coverage provided by other methods, including intrauterine devices (IUD) and sterilization, and how the Malaysia-derived CYP district aggregates provided our best available estimates of district level coverage, in relation to program resource inputs. (My dissertation was completed in 1973, and I was happy to meet that country's request shortly thereafter for several additional copies of my findings and recommendations).

I was not sure where my specific path after completing the doctorate would take me but serendipitously was invited to continue at Michigan in something of a postdoctoral fellowship capacity as a researcher and lecturer. This worked well for me, especially as Carol was enjoying her job responsibilities with the Association for Asian Studies, headquartered in Ann Arbor. My own work involved continuing with some Malaysia research, plus light teaching responsibilities in the University of Michigan School of Public Health (UM-SPH), and with occasional invitations for brief consulting stints in a couple of Asian countries. Meanwhile, global FP was increasingly recognized as an important component of development. Remarkable advances were made in such things as national FP and reproductive health (RH) surveys, while on the United States domestic front states were receiving the new Title 10 federal funding. As was true for several other institutions, this funding helped support academic program expansion and provided funding for research at Michigan. Not entirely by coincidence, 1973 was also the year that USAID, by then active in many countries, decided to use the CYP Index as a major program output measure for assessing some of its own progress.

Simultaneously, FP programs were growing in the United States with major infusions of government funding. More students interested in stateside FP activities were enrolling in our teaching programs to go along with the international growth.

The following year, Michigan invited me to fill in as an assistant professor for one of the tenured professors while he took a sabbatical. CYP was by then included in coursework as one of the quantitative tools for program evaluation. As newer methods including new and often more effective types of IUDs along with short-term injectables and longer-term contraceptive implants were added to the FP arsenal, and as improved data collection on such things as the ages of clients receiving sterilization became available, we and others updated the CYP conversion factors. This was, and continues to this day, to be an ongoing process, in which I became more formally engaged a few years later after I joined CDC.

Before that, however, my Michigan involvement with CYP Index development and use (beyond my own dissertation work) was principally through my teaching, and secondarily through a major study led by Professor Gayl Ness and funded by USAID's Office of Population on factors accounting for different levels of performance across many Asian FP national programs. In this cross-national study in the early 1980s, CYP-derived estimates of contraceptive coverage were one of our main output indicators, which we used with inputs of funding and staffing, along with other factors. To gather this data, we had the advantage that in most of these countries we had some of our former graduate students in positions which allowed them to gather much of the data we requested, well before our own visits to complete the process, and return the data for our planned analyses at Michigan. This resulted in a number of reports and publications documenting our findings, by Gayl Ness and myself, greatly aided by our principal statistician and data manager, Stan Bernstein, whose skills subsequently led him to a highly successful professional career with United Nations Fund for Population Activities (UNFPA).

I joined the CDC's Division of Reproductive Health in September 1983. The division director at that time was Dr. Roger Rochat, whom I'd first met in 1976 when he was still an EIS (epidemic intelligence service) officer, after a presentation I'd made at a session of the American Public Health Association in Miami Beach. I recall the year specifically because the meeting was addressed by the soon–to–be president of the United States, Jimmy Carter, barely out of campaign mode, as he gave a well-received plenary address. (Little could I foresee then that only a bit more than a decade later, and a couple of years after our move from Michigan, my wife, Carol, would accept a position in Atlanta with the still-new Carter Presidential Center, and that she'd remain there in a couple of capacities for over a quarter century until her 2015 retirement).

Within the reproductive health division, I was recruited into the program evaluation branch, at that time headed by Dr. Leo Morris, who'd earlier been much involved in the successful global smallpox eradication campaign (in his case in Brazil). He later completed his own PhD at Michigan, through which I'd first come to know him. By then, his principal interest and studies had switched to reproductive health, both in the United States and overseas, with a particular focus on in population surveys as tools for evaluators and program planners. With my own interest and teaching in statistics and demographic and general program evaluation, and my international background, I fit right in.

Though contraceptive logistics had not been a major focus of my previous international work, I soon found myself in the middle of CDC's assistance to USAID's Office of Population in Washington. There had been longstanding cooperation between USAID's Office of Population and Reproductive Health and the CDC in several areas, including reproductive health (RH) surveys and epidemiological aspects of FP, but also in data-based program evaluation. By 1983, CDC was assisting USAID in several countries in forecasting contraceptive needs. Soon, working with my new CDC colleagues, this became my main focus, helping USAID country missions determine their program needs. In addition to the nuts and bolts of determining countries' needs for different contraceptive supplies, and how to get these to the right places at the right times, we were involved in training professionals on other aspects of their expanding FP duties. At national and international levels, we also worked with USAID and several other agencies in assessing the impact of their programs. In these efforts, CYP measurements again were among the major and still-evolving tools, and CDC and USAID were in the vanguard of these efforts.

There were several aspects to this in which our CDC staff, and I personally, were involved over the next years, particularly with USAID, with which we had an annually renewable funding agreement, especially for support of contraceptive logistics work and secondarily for reproductive health surveys. While the surveys mostly involved women of reproductive age for entire countries, we also assisted with specialized surveys, such as for young adults, both male and female, and sometimes for subnational populations rather than whole countries.

*Tim wearing the Speaker's Cap, proving
all is not serious at these meetings.*

*Tim served both as
speaker and panelist.*

4.　PANEL DISCUSSANTS

4.1　Dr. Tim Johnson, Division of Reproductive Health, CDC, Atlanta, USA

Dr. Tim Johnson addressed the distinguished guests as "colleagues" since every one was present here for a common purpose, which was to establish the appropriate quantities of contraceptives that will be required to prevent unwanted births and sexually transmitted diseases in Bangladesh for the next several years. First of all, he mentioned what a pleasure it was for him to be back in Bangladesh for the first time in 7 years and to see some of the changes. There have been some very remarkable changes and one of the most remarkable is what has happened particularly in the last 15 or so years in the national Family Planning program. Things have really taken off magnificently, he said.

He said that his comments would be fairly brief, as having gone through a process with Dr. Islam and his colleagues, he was of the opinion that it has resulted in very good projections. The base data used for this projection exercise is very good and reliable. Everyone is looking obviously for reasonable and durable projection. He thought Prof. Islam and his colleague Mr. Chakraborty have done a superb job, pulling together different forces and factors and applied them, while maintaining the academic integrity in doing it, which is sometimes difficult and he commended them very much for that.

These projections are indeed based on the best available current evidence from a variety of sources and these have been skillfully put together. The sources don't always agree and then there is a process of reconciliation that has to go on and that's partly a matter of expert opinion. But Dr. Johnson was of the opinion that has been done really quite well.

As has been noted, forecasts start with past experience. One doesn't know what the future reality will be, so one of the needs is to monitor constantly what is actually happening. What is also needed is to establish a mechanism for yearly review of forecast and program performance. What is also needed is to establish a mechanism for yearly review of forecast and program performance about where things stand, and what needs to be done by academicians, program managers and policy makers, to keep abreast of what is happening and to make sure that the right commodities are coming in, to achieve those objectives.

The final main point made by Dr. Johnson was that projections of users and requirements of commodities are only a first step. This has to be followed by very explicit steps to ensure that these products are timely procured and distributed.

He concluded by saying that he felt that the projected requirements presented at the Workshop are demographically and programmatically sound and defensible and would serve policy makers and managers very well as a basis for planning the next steps in the national population efforts.

Dhaka conference with Tim at the head table

On contraceptive logistics, USAID's needs for in-country technical assistance were rapidly overtaking our limited CDC staff capacity to meet the demand. Soon, a large and well-respected private sector group, JSI (formerly the John Snow, Inc.), was contracted by USAID to provide far more extensive support to USAID's global contraceptive efforts. From the start, we developed good collegial relationships with this group, as we had with other nongovernment groups, where CDC's experience and reputation could complement the flexibility and greater funding which the private sector could access. Much of our logistics fieldwork and development of tools for managing all aspects of family planning supplies — from needs forecasting and procurement through warehousing and distribution ultimately to clients — was done jointly over the next years.

CDC in those years took the lead with USAID in updating CYP factors as part of our overall collaboration. During part of this period, after I'd become chief of the FP logistics section in our division, I cochaired with Dr. James Shelton, medical director in USAID's population office, a multi-agency committee which recommended revised CYP factors, especially for supplies provided by USAID. In practice, these in most cases were also accepted as "default" values by other agencies and country programs. The factors were widely disseminated internationally, including through such joint CDC and JSI publications as *Family Planning Logistics Guidelines* and the shorter *Pocket Guide to Managing Contraceptive Supplies*. These also were issued and widely used in Spanish and French versions as part of our joint CDC/JSI contribution with USAID to promoting effective FP and RH programs worldwide.

As a measure of program output, CYP has withstood the test of time rather well. For major methods used around the world, the reasoning underlying the development of factors has not greatly changed from the earliest formulations in the 1960s. The actual factors used have, of course, continued to be updated, to reflect both the greater variety of new methods and changes in user-population characteristics. For example, in the 1960s the Lippes Loop was the main IUD in Pakistan and other early programs, albeit in different sizes. Later IUD factors needed to adjust for different (and longer) protection levels provided by variants of the Copper T. Similarly, the early monthly contraceptive pill cycles yielded to additional formulations, requiring revised factors. New information on use patterns for condoms within different population groups also led to some adjustments. At the start, certain methods that later became widespread (for instance, short-acting hormonal injections and longer-duration implants) were not included. Over time, they were all incorporated into the big picture of contraceptive protection, along with permanent male and female sterilization. This is continuing, and will continue, as an essential part of measuring the effects of programs to assist women, men, and indeed societies in efforts to improve reproductive health as a component of global welfare.

The question of effective measurement and evaluation of family planning programs was a consistent theme throughout my professional life. So was my interest in applying measurement tools to programs. I was fortunate to be present at the beginning of CYP creation, aid in its widespread international adoption and modification over time, and witness its value in the development of effective family planning strategies and outcomes over the course of my decades of involvement in reproductive health.

APPENDIX F

Excerpts from Tim's responses to the CDC's "Logistics Lore Questionnaire," May 2011

Where was the first place you went as a CDC logistics advisor? When was that? What do you remember most about that first trip?

Nigeria in 1983 (for the CDC although I'd done a bit of pre-CDC logistics work in Pakistan, Bangladesh, and Malaysia). What I mainly recall is both the great differences between working in Africa after years of non-logistics contraceptive work in family planning in Asia, and the enthusiasm by both USAID and my fellow consultants (CDC and non-CDC) for helping get the Nigerian program up and running.

Where did you enjoy working most, and why?

Zimbabwe, back in 1984, when it seemed to be making real strides in making contraceptives widely available to both urban and rural women. Unfortunately, this did not last! (Among others I particularly enjoyed are Madagascar, Swaziland, Nepal and Barbados, for a variety of reasons).

What was your most unusual experience in the field?

Getting mugged in Lagos! Fortunately, most of my experiences were much more positive!

What local customs or practices did you encounter that made work in the field more pleasant? Which made work more difficult?

Most of the local staff and officials I worked with were both pleasant and helpful, but the local bureaucratic/administrative environments in which they worked were often major challenges for them and therefore also for me and colleagues. This was true in most countries I've worked in, both in Africa and Asia. Also, a lack of a sense of time, and of meeting deadlines, could wreak havoc with the best laid plans.

Were there any items that you found it was a good idea to take with you in your travels that an inexperienced logistician might not think of?

Imodium! Also, some nonperishable basic food supplies such as trail mix and peanuts, and such items as a flashlight for conducting commodity assessments in electricity-free areas. Paper clips and Post-it notes and spare pencils! A few spare pens to give away.

Did you find any logistics situations that you found to be eye-poppingly different from the ideal logistics setup, or where staff just didn't "get" logistics the way we think it should be done?

Yes, quite often, but on such occasions, I had to remind myself that this was precisely why I was out there, to help overcome those situations!

What were some of the ways people working in the logistics systems had to "make do" in a less-than-ideal world?

Some staff were quite resourceful both in switching users among methods and brands, and in temporary "rationing," and in "borrowing" from the private sector or private agencies in ways they would not want to note in official stock registers!

What regional differences did you find in logistics situations?

In addition to intercountry differences, and the commonly recognized problems of urban-rural differences in contraceptive availability and access, in some countries, including notably Nigeria, there were wide disparities along geographic and ethnic lines, despite efforts to minimize these.

Please share any other stories from your logistics work that you think might be of interest.

Resourcefulness in reaching sites for assessment is a sine qua non for the serious fieldworker. Two examples from personal experience will make the point. In the first, a joint JSI/CDC team used a jeep, followed by a leaky putt-putting riverboat, then a rickshaw, and finally our own legs, to visit a selected field-site in rural Bangladesh.

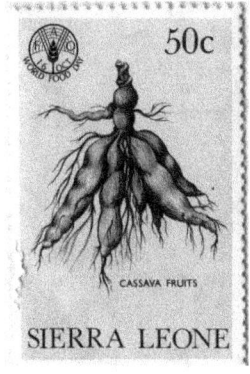

Jeep shown here was on another misadventure, this time in Madagascar with Tim and David Gittelman in 1997

In the second, during the time (1985) Sierra Leone was suffering from both political turmoil and famine, resulting from appalling misgovernment, I was asked to assess Sierra Leone's FP situation. No USAID staff had been up-country for quite a while, as roads were almost impassable in many places, and there was no fuel. Undeterred, and with USAID's blessing, I arranged for the repair of a USAID project's vehicle, which included repair of all four tires. With a driver and the project head, we strapped several large cans of petrol to the vehicle and set off. By the first night, we had visited a few sites (basically no commodities and little recordkeeping) but were developing serious clutch problems. We reached a destination where there was an acceptable rest house, but basically no food. We cadged some from miscellaneous sources. Before we could set out the next morning, a couple of hours were spent on sufficient repairs to allow us to proceed on the rough dirt roads. Red dust filtered in from a hole in the bottom of the vehicle and gradually covered us.

That night, while my Sierra Leone colleague stayed with some friends he knew, I "rested" in a new (and apparently never-before-used) tiny guesthouse at the edge of the little town of Bo. There was no electricity, so no fan. The watchman spoke virtually no English but was able to prepare me a little tea at breakfast, but my dinner consisted of the rations of peanuts and trail mix I'd brought along. For washing, I had about a third of a bucket of water from the well.

I also spent the next night there, but better fed and washed, since the regional coordinator (nursing sister) we'd spent that day with took us to her home, where I was able to rinse off the red residue and refresh myself with ladles of water from her well. Additionally, we located a small but serviceable restaurant. And that night, I lapsed into slumber to the rather relaxing sound of distant "talking drums."

Other observations:

Some advisors become, in my view, too "invested" in the recommendations and advice they give, and become upset with locals who do not accept their expert advice. I've found it helps to be more detached and recognize that while you are providing the best counsel you can, backed by whatever facts and figures you bring to this advice, in the end the call is by the locals, who may have considerations that you simply do not fully grasp. This helps reduce your stress. In simpler language, as far as possible, once you've given your advice, just "go with the flow," so long as this is not obviously going to land them, and you, on the rocks.

It is perhaps worth noting that while much logistics work is undertaken in places tourists would not be likely to pay to visit, this also permits the interested advisor to see things most Americans will simply not experience. First is simply the exposure to other cultures, other peoples, with all that implies. In addition, with little extra effort, one can often take in sights and experiences that can be personally very enriching and satisfying. I could list many such opportunities that have come my way, that in the normal course of events would not have been possible. These experiences, at least for me, have far outweighed the inconveniences and discomforts that are a necessary part of working in very underdeveloped regions of the world, while also providing the professional satisfaction of direct involvement in the terribly important, but too often overlooked, work of helping underserved populations to the means for controlling their fertility and improving their health.

ACKNOWLEDGMENTS

T he gestation period for this volume has been longer than I choose to reveal! Ensuring that it was not stillborn, besides the encouragement of family members, was that of former academic and professional colleagues and several Bruderhof or other community Leavers. From the latter group, I'll only mention by name Ruth Baer-Lambach, whom I met after first arriving in North Dakota, as a teenager. Her Mennonite, Hutterite, and Bruderhof family history provided a perspective that enriched a much later study she and I undertook of what we called a "virtual community" of Leavers.

Further encouragement came from persistent urging by colleagues and friends from my CDC years, both pre- and postretirement. I'll mention just two here. First, Susanna Binzen, herself an inveterate diarist, heard some of my reminiscences and thought they might interest a wider audience than I'd originally envisaged. Most recently she allowed herself to be drafted to serve as a first reader for a section of the book. Second, Mary Serdula, who along with her husband, Ridwan, did her best to save me from further procrastination. In that effort, she had the enthusiastic support of my wife, Carol, (another first reader) who possibly has been even more eager than I for this labor to end with a successful delivery!

My siblings shared their memories, insights, and images as I confirmed portions of our parents' journey. I am grateful to them and to, especially, our sister Elizabeth, the family historian and important first reader of that section.

What started as an idea became an outline, then a series of linked vignettes. The materials were there, but I needed help in knitting it all into a coherent memoir. What to do? Eureka, it was Jennifer "Jiffy" Page to the rescue! Thanks largely to Jiffy's subsequent guidance and the professional contributions of her team members, especially Rick and Ellen, the account of our journeys nears completion.

The final step will be achieved when the volume appears before you, the reader, and you have a chance to share parts of these improbable journeys, filtered through your own life-travel experiences.